Mel Bay Presents

Mastering the Guitar

A COMPREHENSIVE METHOD FOR TODAY'S GUITARIST!

1A

By William Bay & Mike Christiansen

William Bay

Introduction

Mastering the Guitar is an innovative, exciting, and comprehensive way to learn the guitar. Written in notation and tablature, it covers guitar solo and accompaniment styles ranging from Celtic to Classic to Cajun; from Flamenco to fiddle tunes; from Renaissance to Rock to Reggae; from Baroque to Blues to Bluegrass; and from Latin to Country to Jazz. A special feature of this method is that it teaches both flatpicking and fingerstyle solo and accompaniment techniques.

Mike Christiansen

In Book 1A, you will play over 155 solos and duets and more than 140 scale and picking studies, chord etudes and accompaniment pieces in the keys of C, A minor, G, and E minor. A *Technique Studies* book (MB96622, $9.95) and a special double compact disc (MB96620CD, $19.95) are available and are highly recommended! We feel that *Mastering the Guitar* is the most comprehensive approach to guitar technique, repertoire, and performance to be found anywhere. Upon completion of Book 1A, you should proceed immediately to Book 1B.

A recording of the music in this book is now available. The publisher strongly recommends the use of this recording along with the text to insure accuracy of interpretation and ease in learning.

Parts of the Guitar

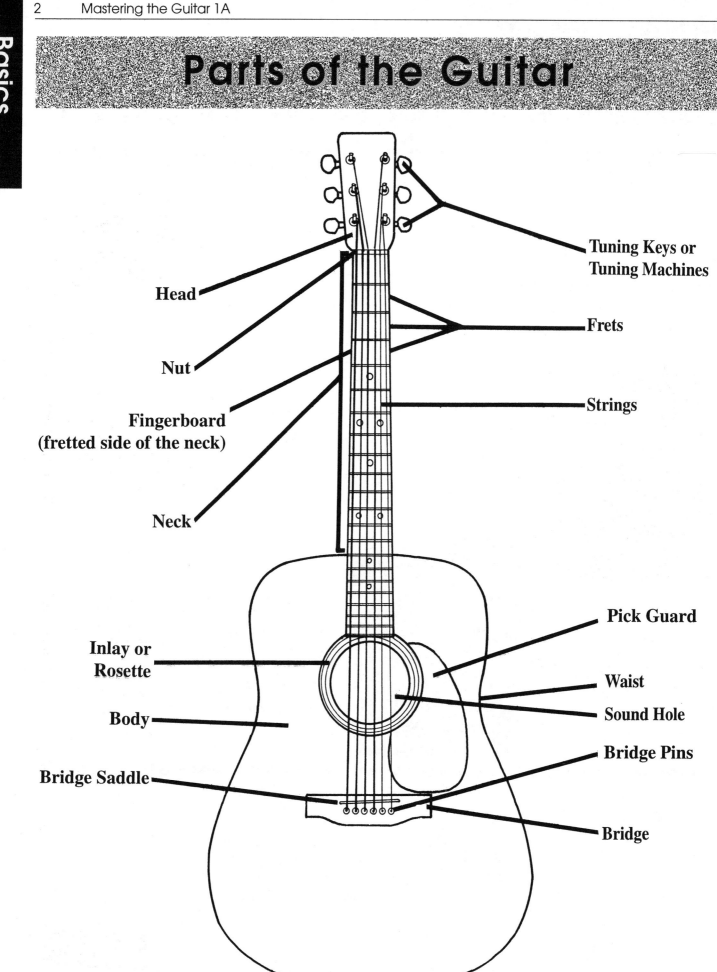

Head

Nut

Fingerboard
(fretted side of the neck)

Neck

Inlay or
Rosette

Body

Bridge Saddle

Tuning Keys or
Tuning Machines

Frets

Strings

Pick Guard

Waist

Sound Hole

Bridge Pins

Bridge

Holding Position

Folk or Jazz Position

Classical Position

If the guitar is held properly, it will feel comfortable to you. Although there are many ways to hold the guitar, there are basically two sitting positions: the folk or jazz and the classical positions. Either position may be used, but for most of the material contained in this book, the folk sitting position is recommended.

In the *folk or jazz sitting position,* the guitar is held with the waist of the guitar resting on the right leg. The side of the guitar sits flat on the leg with the neck extending to the left. The neck should be tilted upward slightly so the left arm *does not* rest on the left leg. Both feet should be flat on the floor, although many guitarists prefer to elevate the right leg by using a footstool. The right arm rests on the top of the guitar just beyond the elbow. The right hand should be placed over and to the back (towards the bridge) of the sound hole. Whether using a pick or the fingers, the right-hand fingers should be bent slightly. The right-hand fingers may touch the top of the guitar, but they should not be stationary. They move when stroking the strings.

In the *classical sitting position,* the left foot is elevated (with a foot stool), and the guitar rests on the left leg. The body of the guitar also rests on the inside of the right leg. The body of the guitar should rest flat on the left leg. The neck of the guitar should be on about a 45° angle. The right arm rests on the top of the guitar just beyond the elbow. The right hand should be placed to the back (towards the bridge) of the sound hole. Lean forward slightly, touching the top/back of the guitar body. Sit so the right foot is pointing forward.

The left hand should be positioned with the thumb touching the back of the guitar neck. Do not bend the thumb forward. The thumb should be vertical, touching the neck at the knuckle. Do not position the thumb parallel with the neck. The palm of the left hand should not touch the guitar neck. The left wrist may bend *slightly,* but be careful not to exaggerate the bend.

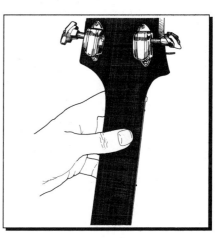

Left-Hand Thumb

When placing a left-hand finger on the string, "square" the finger and push on the string using the tip of the finger. (The fingernails must be short so the tip of the finger can be used.) The finger should be positioned just behind and touching (when possible) the fret wire. Placing the finger too low in the fret may result in a buzz, and placing the finger on top of the fret wire may cause a muted sound. The left-hand knuckles should run parallel with the guitar neck. This makes it possible to reach higher frets with the left-hand third and fourth fingers without turning the wrist. Again, be careful not to bring the left-hand thumb over the top of the guitar neck, and do not touch the guitar neck with the palm of the hand. When pushing on the string, it is as though the guitar neck and string are being pinched between the thumb and finger.

Push the string firmly enough to get a sound, but don't over push. To determine the correct amount of pressure, touch the string with the left-hand finger and gradually apply pressure. Pick the string over and over. When a clear sound occurs, that's the amount of pressure to use.

Fingering Notes

Basics

Rest your right-hand thumb on the first (the smallest) string and stroke the open string (open means no left-hand fingers are pushing on the string) downward. Make sure the right-hand wrist moves, and the arm moves slightly from the elbow. The right-hand fingers may touch the top of the guitar, but they should move when the string is played. Try to have a relaxed feeling in the right hand. Go straight down with the thumb when stroking the string. Next, with the right-hand thumb, play the second string open. When playing a string other than the first string, the thumb should go straight down and rest upon (but not play) the next smallest string. In classic guitar playing, this is called a **rest stroke.**

Strumming refers to playing three or more strings so the strings sound simultaneously. To practice the strumming action, rest the right-hand thumb on the fourth string and strum four strings. Using a down stroke, let the right hand fall quickly across the strings so they sound at the same time. The right-hand wrist and arm move with the action.

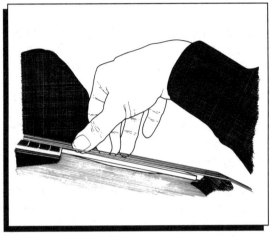

When playing fingerstyle (without a pick), the position of the right hand is very important to achieving a good sound. The right hand should be placed over the rear (towards the bridge) portion of the sound hole. The right-hand fingers should be relaxed and curled in the same manner in which they would be if you were walking. When stroking the string, the tip of the thumb and/or fingers should strike the string first, followed by the tip of the fingernail. This motion should happen quickly so it sounds as if the finger and nail are striking the string at the same time.

Avoid bending the thumb at the first knuckle (the knuckle closest to the nail). Bend the thumb from the joint closest to the palm of the hand. The first knuckle of the fingers should not bend. The movement of the fingers should be restricted to the joint closest to the palm of the right hand and the middle knuckle. When picking up with the fingers, use an up and slightly outward motion. Play one string at a time, and avoid hitting the string next to the one being played. Be careful not to pull the string away from the guitar. This will cause a "flappy, twang" sound. When picking with the thumb, go down and out slightly. Again, avoid pulling the string away from the guitar, and after striking a string, avoid hitting the string next to it.

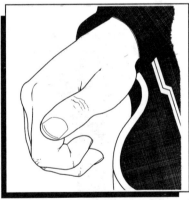

To hold the pick correctly, first, bend the right-hand index finger. The other fingers of the right hand also bend, but not as much as the index finger.

The pick is placed on the end of the index finger with the pointed part of the pick aiming away from the index finger.

The thumb is placed over the pick, covering $2/3$ to $3/4$ of the pick.

To place the right hand (with the pick) in playing position, rest the pick on the first string. The pick should be tilted upward slightly, rather than at a direct right angle to the string. The pick should stroke the string just over and to the back (towards the bridge) of the sound hole. Pick the first string down. The right-hand wrist should move slightly when the string is played, and the right arm should move slightly from the elbow. When playing strings other than the first, after stroking the string, the pick should rest on the next smallest string. This action is a type of **rest stroke,** which is commonly used in fingerstyle playing, and will generate a richer and fuller tone than picking with an outward motion will. Try playing each of the strings using this type of motion.

To get the feel of strumming with the pick, rest the pick on the fourth string and strum four strings down. Be sure to have a relaxed right hand. Move the wrist and arm slightly when doing the strumming. When picking a single string, or strumming, upward, the pick is tilted down slightly so the pick will glide across the strings, rather than "bite" or snag them.

Tuning

There are several methods which can be used to tune the guitar. One way to tune the guitar is to tune it to itself. You can tune the first string of the guitar to a piano, pitch pipe, tuning fork, or some other instrument, and then match the strings to each other. To do this, use the following steps:

▶ 1. Tune the first open string to an E note. (Remember, open means that no left-hand fingers are pushing on the string.) You can use a piano, pitch pipe, tuning fork, or another instrument. If you use a tuning fork, use an "E" tuning fork. Hold the fork at the bass and tap the fork on your knee, or something else, to get the fork to vibrate. Then, touch the bass of the fork near the bottom of the bridge of the guitar. The pitch which will sound is the pitch the first string should have when the string is played open.

▶ 2. After the first string is tuned, place a left-hand finger on the second string in the fifth fret. Play the first and second strings together. They should be the same pitch. If not, adjust the second string to match the first.

▶ 3. Place a finger on the third string in the fourth fret. The third string should now sound the same as the second string open. If not, adjust the third string.

▶ 4. Place a finger on the fourth string in the fifth fret. The fourth string, fifth fret should sound the same as the third string open.

▶ 5. Place a finger on the fifth string, fifth fret. This should sound the same as the fourth string open.

▶ 6. Place a finger on the sixth string, fifth fret. The sixth string, fifth fret should sound the same as the fifth string, open.

The diagram below shows where the fingers are placed to tune the guitar to itself.

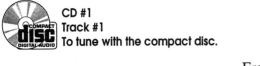

CD #1
Track #1
To tune with the compact disc.

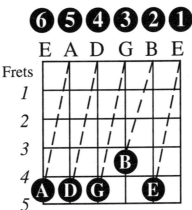

Another common method of tuning is the use of an electronic tuner. Tuners utilize lights (LEDs) or Vu meters to indicate if a string is sharp or flat. Tuners have built in microphones or electric guitars can be plugged in directly. Follow the instructions provided with the tuner. If the tuner does not respond to playing a string, make sure you are playing the correct string and, if it is adjustable, the tuner is set for that particular string. Sometimes on the lower notes, the tuner won't function properly. If this happens, try playing the harmonic on the twelfth fret of the string. To do this, place a left-hand finger on the string over the twelfth fretwire. Touch (do not push) the string very lightly. Pick the string. A note should be heard which will have a "chime" type of effect. This is a harmonic. It will ring longer if the left-hand finger is moved away from the string soon after it is picked. The electric tuner will most likely respond to this note.

Reading the Music Diagrams

Basics

The music in this book will be written using chord diagrams, tablature, and standard notation.

Chord diagrams will be used to illustrate chords and scales. With the chord diagrams, the vertical lines represent the strings on the guitar, with the first string being on the right. The horizontal lines represent frets, with the first fret being on the top. Dots, or numbers, on the lines show the placement of left-hand fingers. The numbers on, or next to the dots indicate which left-hand finger to use. A diamond may be used to indicate the placement of the root of the chord or scale. **Root** refers to a note which has the same letter name as the chord or scale.

A zero above a string indicates the string is to be played open (no left-hand fingers are pushing on the string). An "X" above a string indicates that string is not to be played, or that the string is to be muted by tilting one of the left-hand fingers and touching the string lightly.

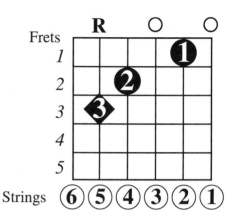

Left-Hand Fingers

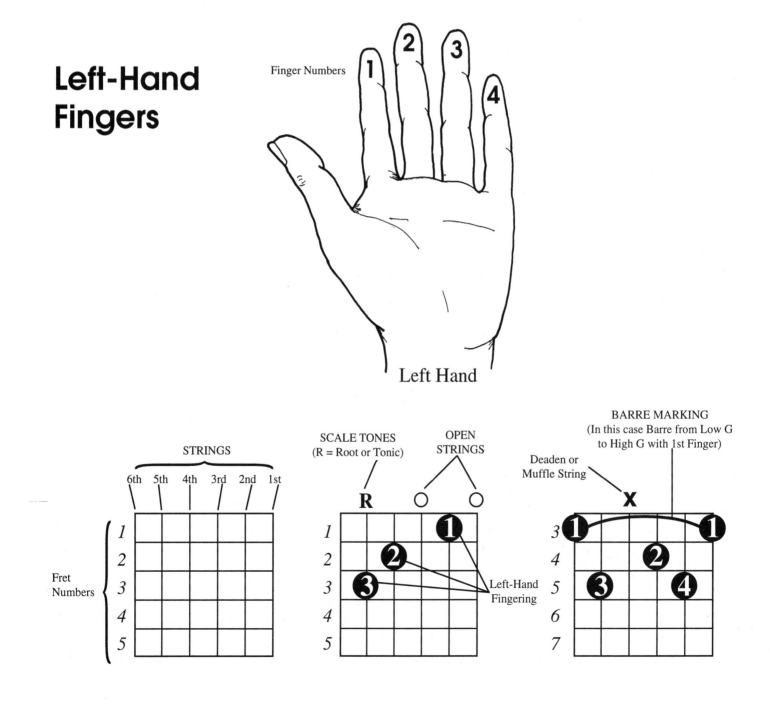

Left Hand

First Warm-Up

To become familiar with the feel of the guitar, and to develop coordination, do the following warm-up exercise:

Step 1

Begin by playing the first string, open. **Open** means no left-hand fingers are pushing on the string.

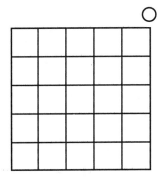

Step 2

Next, play the first string, first fret. The left-hand first finger should be pushing on the string. Be sure to get a good, clear sound.

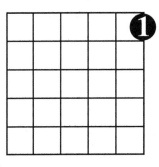

Step 3

Next, play the first string, second fret. The left-hand second finger should be used to push on the second fret.

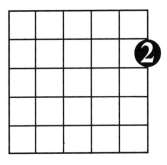

Step 4

Next, play the first string, third fret, using the left-hand third finger.

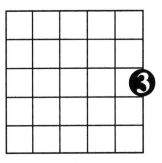

Step 5

Finally, play the first string, fourth fret, using the left-hand fourth finger.

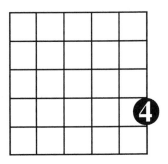

Now, play these same notes in the reverse order (4-3-2-1), still on the first string. Repeat this exercise several times up and down the fingerboard. Notice that the same number left-hand finger is used as the fret number. After doing the exercise several times on the first string, repeat the same sequence on each string.

Simple Chords

If three or more strings are played at the same time, this is called a ***chord.*** Drawn on the diagrams below are the simple G and C chords. These chords may also be referred to as G major and C major. Major chords are those which are written with a letter name only. That is, they will not have an "m" or numbers written after the letter name. Remember, zero above a string indicates the string is to be played open, and an "X" indicates the string is not to be played. Be careful to use the correct left-hand finger. Use the right-hand thumb or a pick to strum the chords. Be sure to strum straight down using a combination of the wrist and elbow.

These two signs, / and ⌡ , are called strum bars. They indicate the chord is to be strummed down one time. This sign, ⊓, when written above a strum bar, ⅂, confirms that the strum is to be strummed down. Up strums will be presented later in this book.

Practice playing the G and C chords. Get a clear sound out of each string.

Practice changing from one chord to the next. A technique which will help you change chords quickly is to keep your right hand going when changing chords. At first, you might play open strings between the chord changes because it will be difficult to change quickly.

But, eventually, the left hand will catch up to the right and the "open-string fill" will go away because you can change chords quickly.

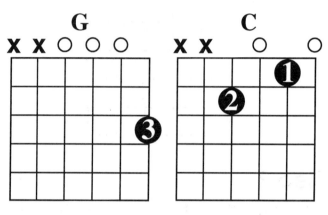

The following exercise uses **G** and **C** chords. Strum each chord the number of times indicated by the strum bars.

G	C	G	C
/ / / / / / / /	/ / / / / / / /	/ / / / / / / /	/ / / / / / / /

G	C	G	C	G
/ / / /	/ / / /	/ / / /	/ / / /	/ / / /

The next chord to learn is simple **G7.**

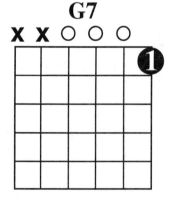

Play the following exercise which contains simple G7.

C	G7	C	G7
/ / / / / / / /	/ / / / / / / /	/ / / /	/ / / /

C	G	G7	C
/ / / / / / / /	/ / / /	/ / / /	/ / / / / / / /

Playing Chords to Measured Music

Remember, if a song is in 4/4 time, there are four counts in each measure. In 3/4 time, there are three counts in each measure. If you don't know this, refer to the section in this book on "Reading Standard Notation" (pg. 11).

For 4/4 time, the simplest strum is to play down four times in each measure. This accompaniment, though simple, will work for many songs.

Play the following exercise strumming down four times in each measure. If a chord name is not written above a measure, continue playing the last written chord through that measure.

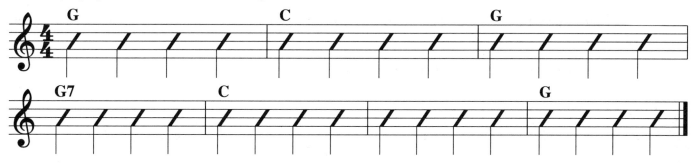

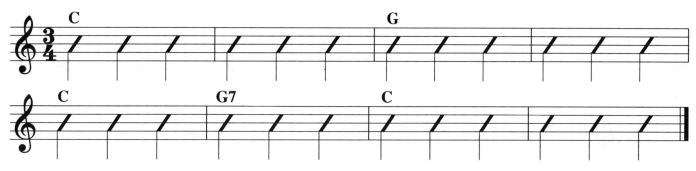

Because the next exercise is in 3/4, you should strum down three times in each measure.

Practice playing the following song which is in 4/4. Strum down four times in each measure. When playing the chords to a song from music like this, do not be concerned with the notes. Only be concerned with the chord names, the number of measures each chord gets, and the number of beats in each measure.

Marianne

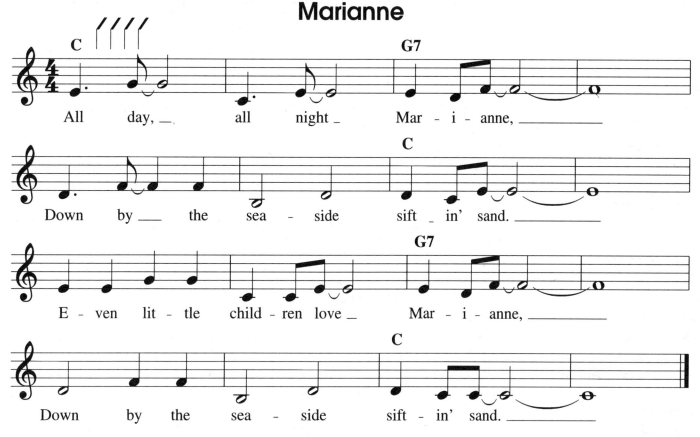

All day, ___ all night ___ Mar - i - anne, _____

Down by ___ the sea - side sift ___ in' sand. _____

E - ven lit - tle child - ren love ___ Mar - i - anne, _____

Down by the sea - side sift - in' sand. _____

Basics

This sign, 𝄍, is a **half-note strum.** It indicates that a chord gets two beats. Strum the chord down on the first beat and let the chord ring through the second beat.

Play the following exercise which contains **half-note strums.**

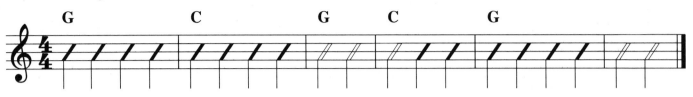

This sign, ⫽, is a **whole-note strum.** It indicates the chord gets four beats. Strum the chord on the first beat and let it ring for three more beats.

Play the following exercise containing **whole-note** and **half-note strums.**

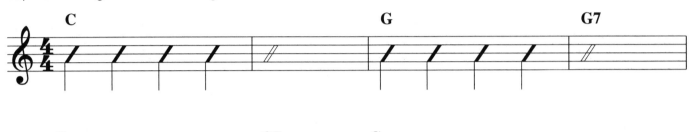

Definition of Guitar Terms

Up the Neck.	Toward the body.
Down the Neck.	Away from the body.
Plectrum.	The small device made of nylon or plastic which is held between the thumb and first finger and is used to strike the strings. It is also referred to as a "pick."
Pick.	a) The act of stroking the string to produce a sound. b) Another name for the plectrum.
Open.	No fingers of the left hand pushing on the strings while the right hand is stroking the strings or string.
Chord.	More than two notes sounded at the same time.
Strum.	Stroking more than two strings at the same time so the strings vibrate simultaneously.
Lower Strings.	The larger strings on the guitar.
Higher Strings.	The smaller strings on the guitar.
1st String.	The smallest string on the guitar.
6th String.	The largest string on the guitar.
Acoustic Guitar.	Any non-electric guitar.
Electric Guitar.	A guitar which has magnetic "pick-ups" which convert the vibration of the strings into a current. This current is then passed through a chord to an amplifier.
Amp or Amplifier.	The device which electrically amplifies an electric guitar.
Meter.	The number of beats or counts per measure.
Tempo.	The speed of counts per measure.
6-String Chord.	A chord which may have all 6 strings strummed or picked.
5-String Chord.	A chord which may have 5 strings (all but the 6th string) played.
4-String Chord.	A chord which may have 4 strings (all but the 6th and 5th strings) played.
Accompaniment Pattern.	A series of strums or a series of strings picked in a specific pattern. Each pattern takes one measure to complete and is repeated every measure.
Strum Pattern.	A series of down and up strums combined to form a rhythmic pattern.
Fingerstyle.	Using the fingers of the right hand to stroke the strings rather than using a pick.

Reading Standard Notation

The Staff

Music is written on a *staff* consisting of *five lines* and *four spaces.* The lines and spaces are numbered upward as shown.

5TH LINE —————————————————————————————————
4TH LINE —————————————— 4TH SPACE ——————————
3RD LINE —————————————— 3RD SPACE ——————————
2ND LINE —————————————— 2ND SPACE ——————————
1ST LINE —————————————— 1ST SPACE ——————————

The lines and spaces are named after letters of the alphabet.

The *lines* are named as follows:

5 ———————————————————— (F) ————
4 ————————————————— (D) —————————
3 ————————————— (B) ———————————————
2 ————————— (G) ———————————————————   **Fine**
1 ————— (E) ———————————————————————   **Does**
                       Boy

   Good

The letters can easily be remembered by the sentence — **E**very

The letter-names of the *spaces* are:

4   E
3   C
2   A
1   F   They spell the word **F-A-C-E.**

The musical alphabet has seven letters – **A B C D E F G.**

The *staff* is divided into measures by vertical lines called *bars.*

                  BAR   BAR

**DOUBLE BARS
MARK THE END
OF A SECTION OR
STRAIN OF MUSIC.**

      MEASURE   MEASURE   MEASURE

The Clef

This sign is the treble or G clef.

All guitar music will be written in this clef.

The second line of the treble clef is known as the G line. Many people call the treble clef the G clef because it circles around the G line.

Notes

THIS IS A NOTE:

A NOTE HAS THREE PARTS. THEY ARE:

The HEAD
The STEM
The FLAG

NOTES MAY BE PLACED IN THE STAFF,   ABOVE THE STAFF,

AND BELOW THE STAFF.

A note will bear the name of the line or space it occupies on the staff.
The location of a note in, above, or below the staff will indicate the pitch.

PITCH: the height or depth of a tone.
TONE: a musical sound.

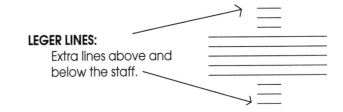

LEGER LINES:
Extra lines above and
below the staff.

Types of Notes

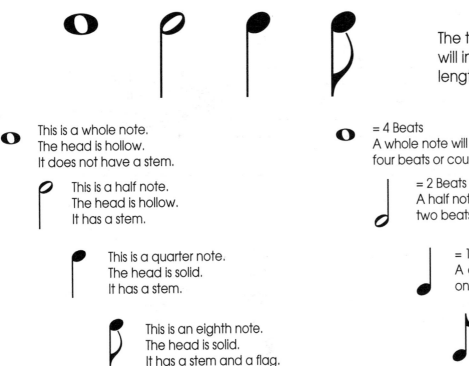

The type of note
will indicate the
length of its sound.

𝅝 This is a whole note.
The head is hollow.
It does not have a stem.

𝅗𝅥 This is a half note.
The head is hollow.
It has a stem.

𝅘𝅥 This is a quarter note.
The head is solid.
It has a stem.

𝅘𝅥𝅮 This is an eighth note.
The head is solid.
It has a stem and a flag.

𝅝 = 4 Beats
A whole note will receive
four beats or counts.

𝅗𝅥 = 2 Beats
A half note will receive
two beats or counts.

𝅘𝅥 = 1 Beat
A quarter note will receive
one beat or count.

𝅘𝅥𝅮 = $\frac{1}{2}$ Beat
An eighth note will receive
one-half beat or count.
(2 for 1 beat)

Rests

A **rest** is a sign used to designate a period of silence. This period of silence will be of the same duration of time as the note to which it corresponds.

This is an eighth rest.

This is a quarter rest.

Half rest.
(Half rests lie on the line.)

Whole rest.
(Whole rests hang down from the line.)

Notes

Whole 4 Counts	Half 2 Counts	Quarter 1 Count	Eighth 2 for 1 Count

Rests

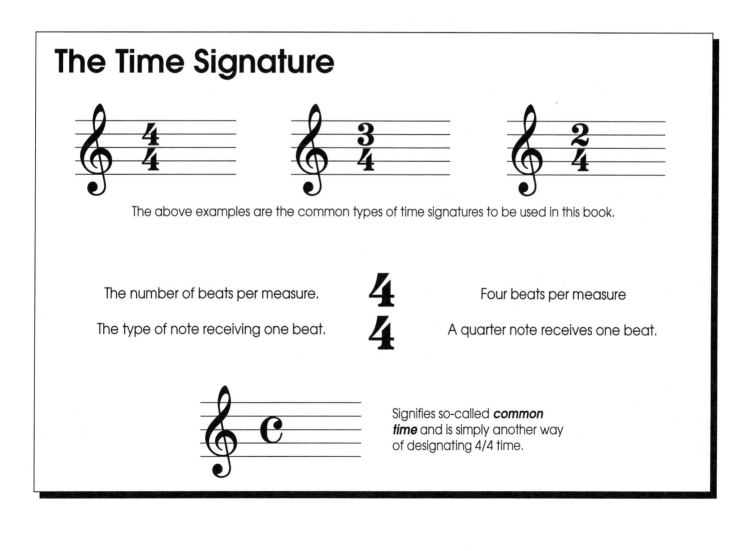

The Time Signature

The above examples are the common types of time signatures to be used in this book.

The number of beats per measure.

4

Four beats per measure

The type of note receiving one beat.

4

A quarter note receives one beat.

Signifies so-called **common time** and is simply another way of designating 4/4 time.

Basics

Our First Note

E

The first string on the guitar is called the high E String. **Our first note is E-open 1st string.**

(Open)

Unless otherwise indicated, use a pick to play the exercises and solos in this book. Use a downstroke to play quarter, half, and whole notes.

E Study #1

(Use a pick to play the following studies)

Pick: Down Down Down Down

Count: 1 2 3 4 1 2 3 4 1 2 3 4 1 2 3 4

E Study #2

Pick:

Count: 1 2 3 4 1 2 3 4

E Study #3

Count: 1 2 3 4 1 2 3 4

E Study #4

Count: 1 2 3 4 1 2 3 4 1 2 3 4 1 2 3 4

E Study #5

Pick:

Count: 1 2 3 4

$\frac{3}{4}$ Time

In 3/4 time we have three beats per measure.

E in $\frac{3}{4}$ Time

Pick: down down down

Count: 1   2   3   1   2   3

#2

Count: 1   2   3   1   2 3

#3

Count: 1   2 3   1 2   3

Eighth Notes/Alternate Picking

Shown below are eighth notes and their time values:

Eighth Notes get $^1/_2$ beat if the bottom number of the time signature is a four.

One beat. The beat is divided equally into two parts. Count the first eighth note as the beat in the measure on which it happens, and count the second eighth note as "and."

When two eighth notes are connected, the first is played using a downstroke, ⊓ , and the second is played using an upstroke, ∨ . This is called *alternate picking.* This technique is used regardless of the position or the string on which the note is played. **Use alternate picking on all eighth notes throughout this book, unless otherwise indicated.** When tapping your foot, the first eighth note is played down when the foot is down, and the second eighth note is played up when the foot is up.

Play the following exercise which contains eighth notes, alternate picking, and the E note on the first string. Be sure to count and tap your foot.

Hiking Up the Mountain

Say: Hi-king up the moun-tain, Hi-king up the moun-tain

Try clapping the rhythm while you say the rhythmic phrase.

Don't Step on Alligators!

(Say and Play)

Don't step on al-li-ga-tors! etc.

Cruising Down the Super Highway

(Say and Play)

Crui-sing down the su-per high-way, etc.

Start Picking Up and Down

(Say and Play)

Start pick-ing up and down, etc.

A New Note:

F

1st Fret
1st Finger
1st String

Press the fingers down firmly behind the frets.
Never place the finger directly on the fretwire.

Note that the numbers
of the fret and finger
are identical.

Play F

E-F

E-F in $\frac{3}{4}$ Time

Basics

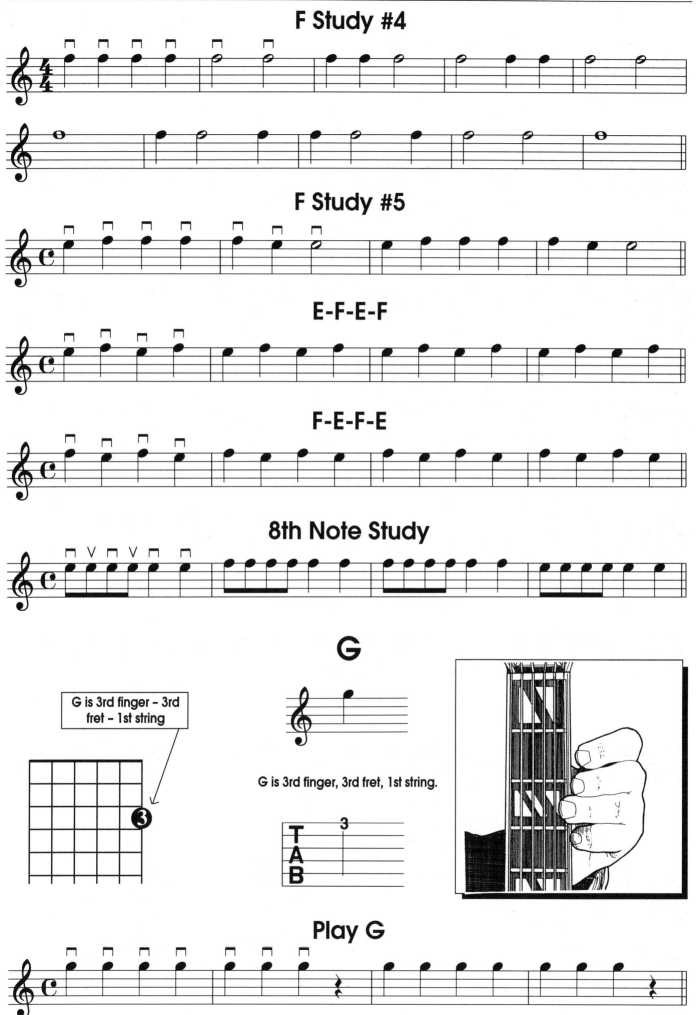

F Study #4

F Study #5

E-F-E-F

F-E-F-E

8th Note Study

G

G is 3rd finger – 3rd fret – 1st string

G is 3rd finger, 3rd fret, 1st string.

Play G

Basics

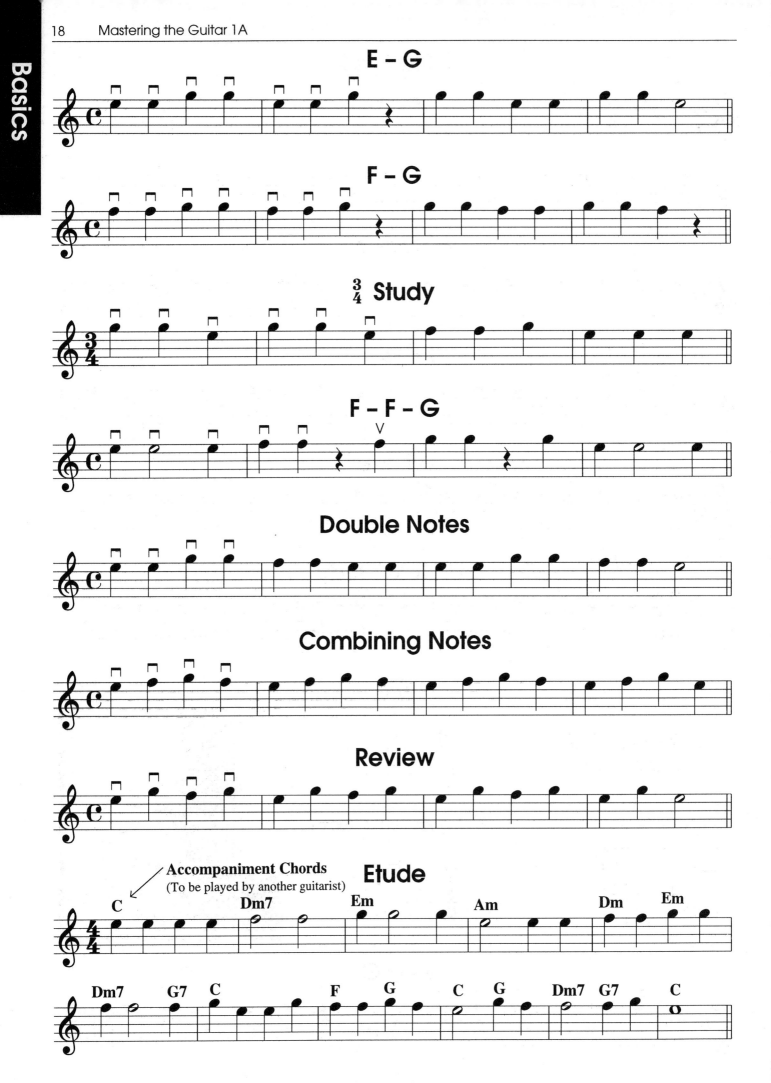

E – G

F – G

¾ Study

F – F – G

Double Notes

Combining Notes

Review

Etude

Accompaniment Chords
(To be played by another guitarist)

1st String Studies

8th Note Rhythm

Study #2

Picking Study

Time and Picking Study

Speed Study

Learning to Read Tablature

Tablature is a way of writing guitar music which tells you where to find notes. In tablature:

Lines = Strings
Numbers = Frets

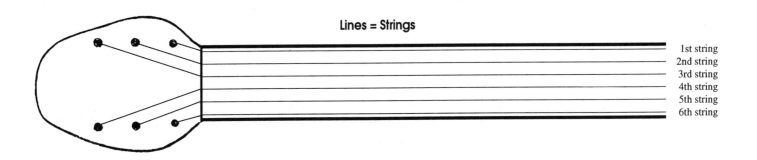

Lines = Strings

1st string
2nd string
3rd string
4th string
5th string
6th string

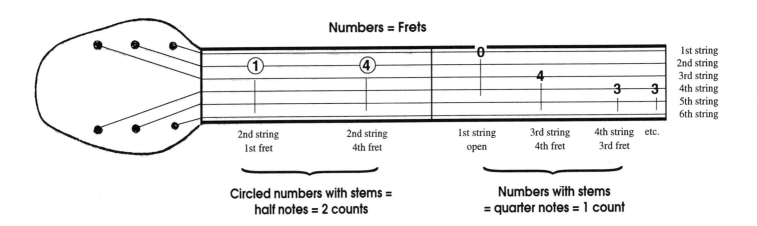

Numbers = Frets

1st string
2nd string
3rd string
4th string
5th string
6th string

| 2nd string 1st fret | 2nd string 4th fret | 1st string open | 3rd string 4th fret | 4th string 3rd fret | etc. |

Circled numbers with stems =
half notes = 2 counts

Numbers with stems
= quarter notes = 1 count

Playing Several Notes at Once

When numbers appear right above one another, more than one note is played at the same time.

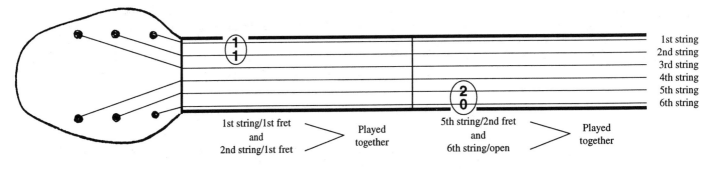

1st string
2nd string
3rd string
4th string
5th string
6th string

1st string/1st fret
and
2nd string/1st fret   > Played together

5th string/2nd fret
and
6th string/open   > Played together

Circled numbers without stems = whole notes = 4 counts

Tab Solos (Using 1st String and Open 6th String)

Basics

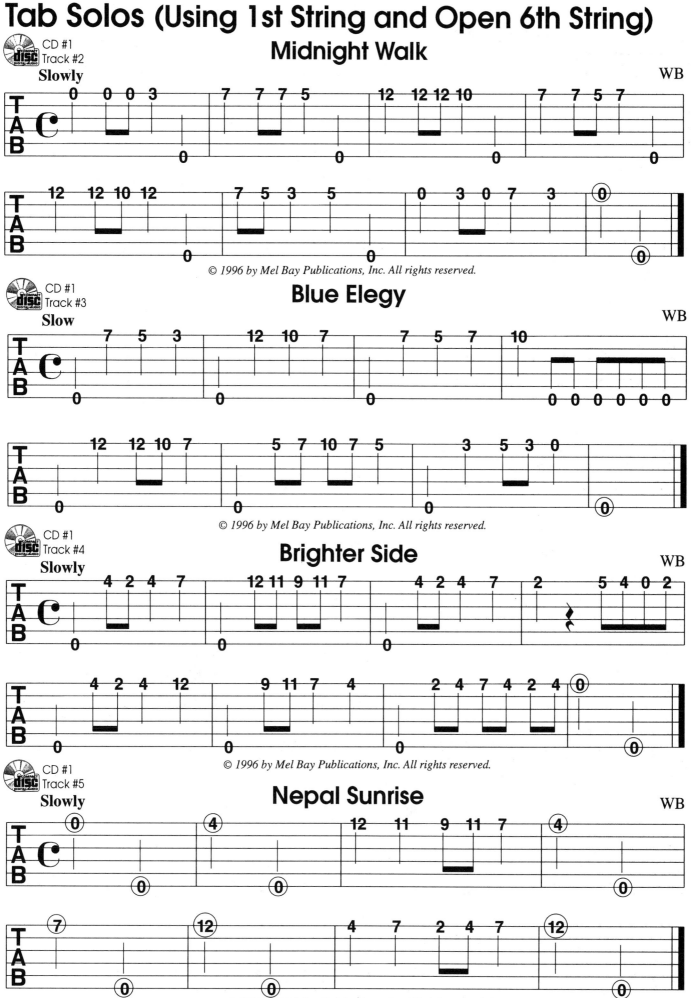

Basics

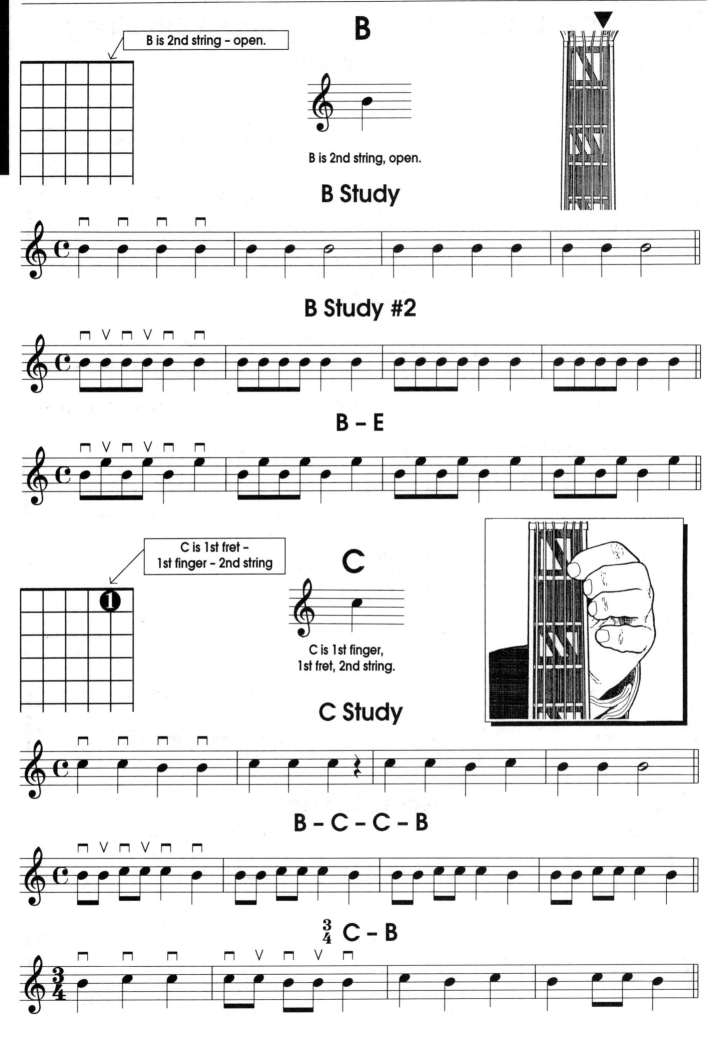

B is 2nd string – open.

B

B is 2nd string, open.

B Study

B Study #2

B – E

C is 1st fret –
1st finger – 2nd string

C

C is 1st finger,
1st fret, 2nd string.

C Study

B – C – C – B

¾ C – B

D

D is 3rd finger – 3rd Fret – 2nd string

D is 3rd finger, 3rd fret, 2nd string.

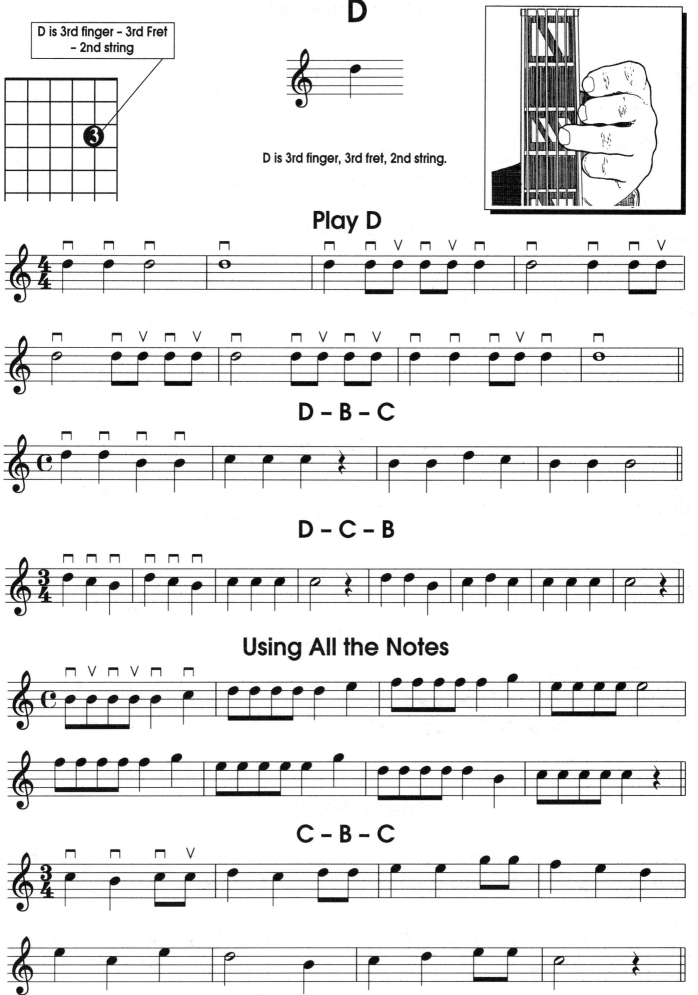

Play D

D – B – C

D – C – B

Using All the Notes

C – B – C

Tab Solos

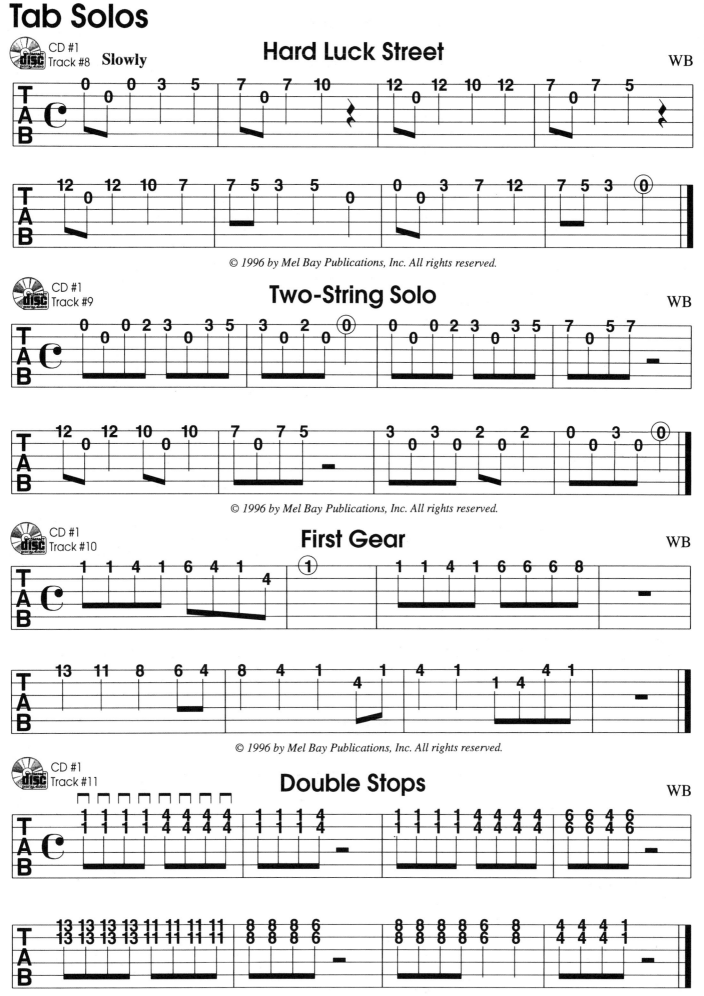

Basics

The Tie

A *tie* is a curved line that connects two notes of the *same* pitch. *With a tie, you pick only the first note.*

If the first end of the two eighth notes is tied  don't play the first note, and play the second note using an upstroke.

Let this eighth note ring through the time value of the next eighth note.

Practice the following exercise containing ties.

Dotted Half Note

A dotted half note receives 3 beats.

Study

Cmaj7   Dm7   C   Dm7   C G C

Dotted Half Strum

This is a dotted half strum: . Like the dotted half note, it gets three beats. Strum the chord on the first beat and let it ring for two more beats.

Play the following exercise which contains a dotted half strum.

C   G7   C G7 C

The Slur/Hammer-on/Pull-off

A **slur** is a curved line that connects two or more notes of a different pitch. *When a slur occurs, pick only the first note.* The remaining notes are fingered but not picked. A slur going up in pitch is sometimes called a **hammer-on.** A slur going down in pitch is sometimes called a **pull-off.**

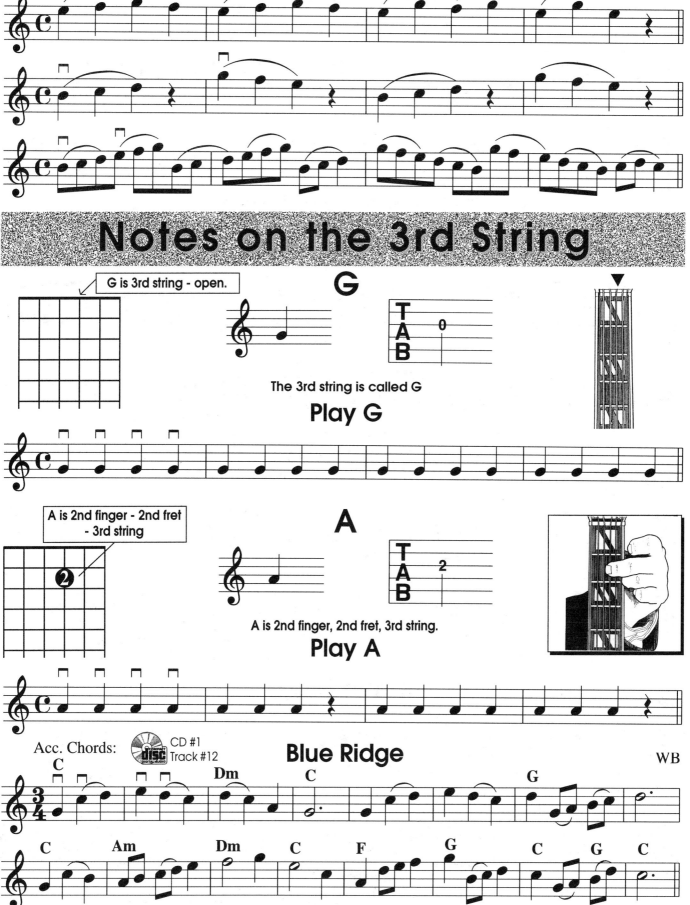

Notes on the 3rd String

G is 3rd string - open.

G

The 3rd string is called G

Play G

A is 2nd finger - 2nd fret - 3rd string

A

A is 2nd finger, 2nd fret, 3rd string.

Play A

Acc. Chords: CD #1 Track #12

Blue Ridge

WB

C   Dm   C   G

C   Am   Dm   C   F   G   C   G   C

Basics

Review of the First 3 Strings

Running the Strings

WB

Kentucky Rise

CD #1
Track #13

WB

Celtic Dawn

CD #1
Track #14

WB

Swamp Buggy

CD #1
Track #15

WB

* Pick-up notes are notes leading into the downbeat of the first measure of a song.

Solos on the First 3 Strings

Renaissance Dance

CD #1 Track #16

WB

Chanson

CD #1 Track #17

WB

© 1996 by Mel Bay Publications, Inc. All rights reserved.

Sourwood Mountain

CD #1 Track #18

Fiddle Tune

Oh, Sinner Man

CD #1 Track #19

Southern Spiritual

Arkansas Traveler

CD #1 Track #20

American Fiddle Tune

Basics

The Slide

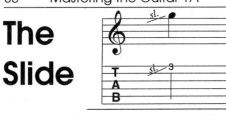

A **slide** is indicated with a *slanted line* and an "*sl.*" written before a note. If the line slants up to the note, slide from two frets below to the written note. If the line slants down to the note, slide from two frets above to the written note. If two notes are connected with a slanted line, pick the first note and without picking the string again, slide the same finger on the string to the second note.

Tab Solos on the First 3 Strings

Remember: The lines show what string you play. The numbers show what fret to play.

Bottleneck Joe

CD #1 Track #21   WB

Slowly, Blues feeling

Past Midnight

CD #1 Track #22   WB

Very slow blues

Hills of Eire

CD #1 Track #23   WB

Medium tempo
Acc. Chords

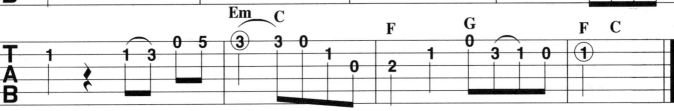

E Minor

Em

The chord drawn at left is E minor. **Minor** chords are written with an *m* or a *dash (-)* next to the chord letter name.

Practice the following exercise which contains E minor.

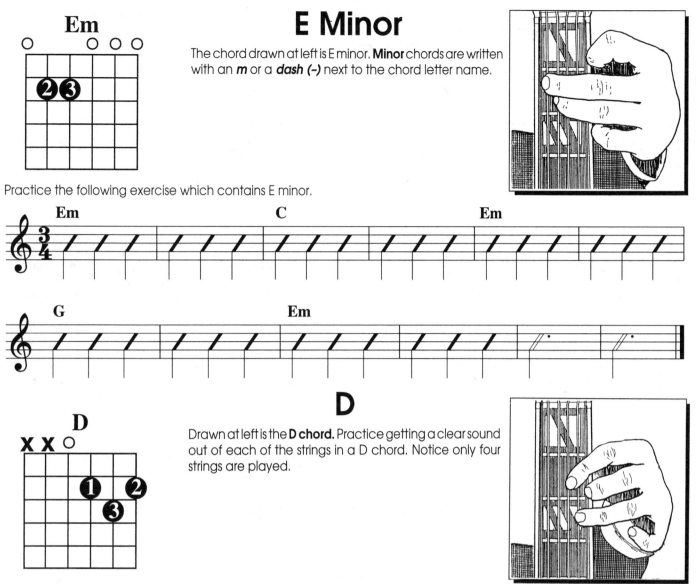

D

D

X X O

Drawn at left is the **D chord.** Practice getting a clear sound out of each of the strings in a D chord. Notice only four strings are played.

Practice the following exercises which contain some D chords. Notice the use of rests in this exercise.

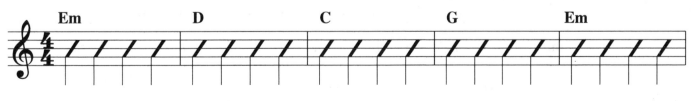

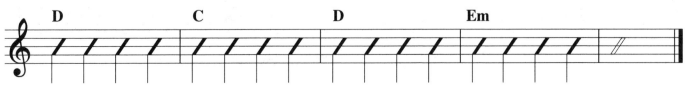

Basics

Practice the following songs using the chords you have learned so far. Above the first measure in each song is written the number of times to strum in each measure.

The Cuckoo

Oh, the cuck - oo _____ She's a pretty bird, _____ She sings _____ as she flies, _____ And she ne - ver _____ hol - lers cuck - oo _____ 'Til the fourth _____ of Ju - ly. _____

> **>** : This is an **accent mark.** When it is placed above a note or a strum bar, play that note or strum slightly louder.

Sweet Sunny South

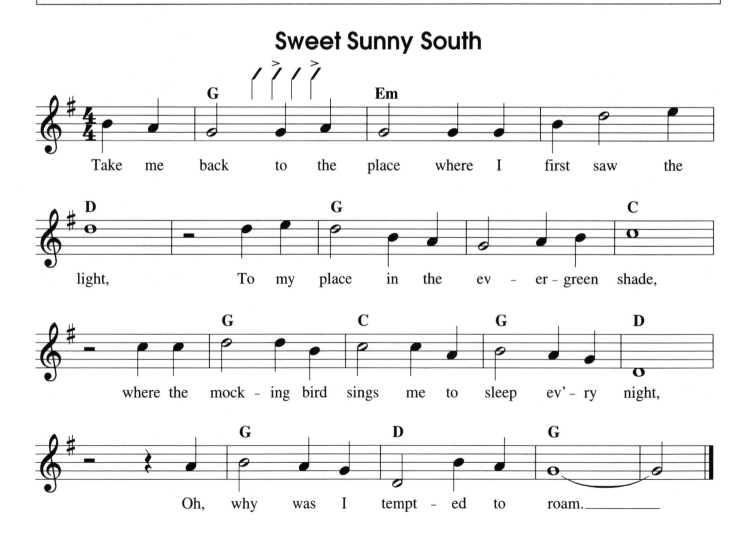

Take me back to the place where I first saw the light, To my place in the ev - er - green shade, where the mock - ing bird sings me to sleep ev' - ry night, Oh, why was I tempt - ed to roam. _____

Full G, G7, and C Chords

Drawn below are the full **G, G7, and C chords.** These full chords will sound better than the simple chords and should be used from here on throughout this book. To get a clear sound out of each string, keep the knuckles square and use the tips of the fingers. On the G chord, the numbers in parenthesis are an optional fingering.

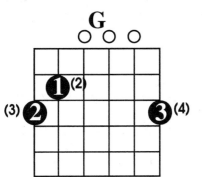
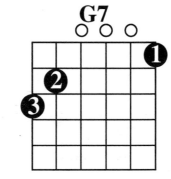
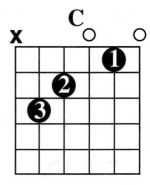

Practice the following exercises using full chords.

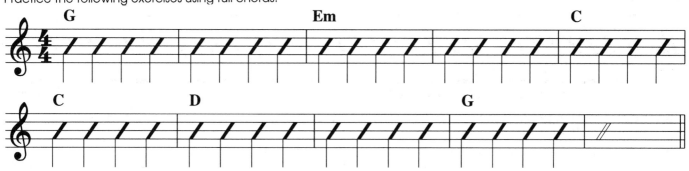

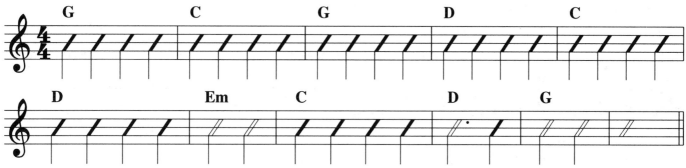

Practice strumming the chords to the following song using full chords.

Will the Circle Be Unbroken?

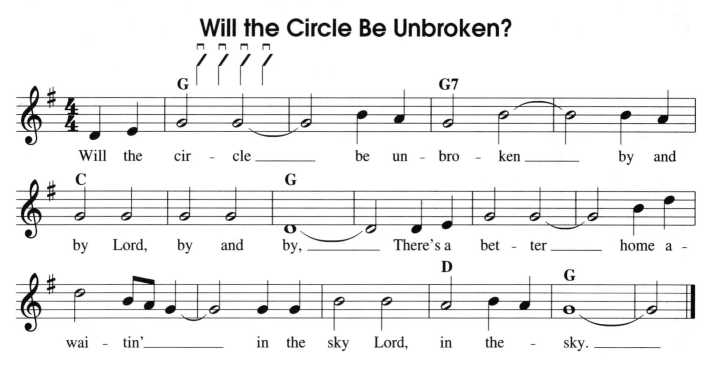

Will the cir - cle _____ be un - bro - ken _____ by and

by Lord, by and by, _____ There's a bet - ter _____ home a -

wai - tin' _____ in the sky Lord, in the - sky. _____

Basics

Strum Patterns

Like eighth notes, when two strum bars are connected with a beam, 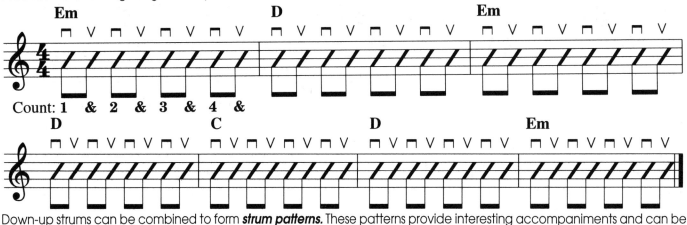, two strums are played in one beat. Usually, the first strum is down, and the second is strummed up, . The down-up strum is counted the same as two eighth notes (i.e. "one-and"). As with the down strums, the strumming may be done with a pick, the right-hand thumb, or the first finger. When strumming up, only the first (smallest) two or three strings should be strummed. The up strum is done quickly with an up and outward motion.

Practice the following using down-up strums.

Down-up strums can be combined to form **strum patterns.** These patterns provide interesting accompaniments and can be used to play many songs. One pattern which can be used to accompany songs in 4/4 is: .

This pattern can be used to play each measure of any song in 4/4. The songs and exercises in this book which are to be strummed will have strum patterns written above (or in) the first measure. That pattern should be used in each measure of the song, unless otherwise indicated. It's important to realize that these patterns can not only be used to play the songs in this book, but they can also be applied to songs in 4/4 and 3/4 from sheet music and/or songbooks.

Practice the following exercise and song repeating the strum pattern which is written above (or in) the first measure.

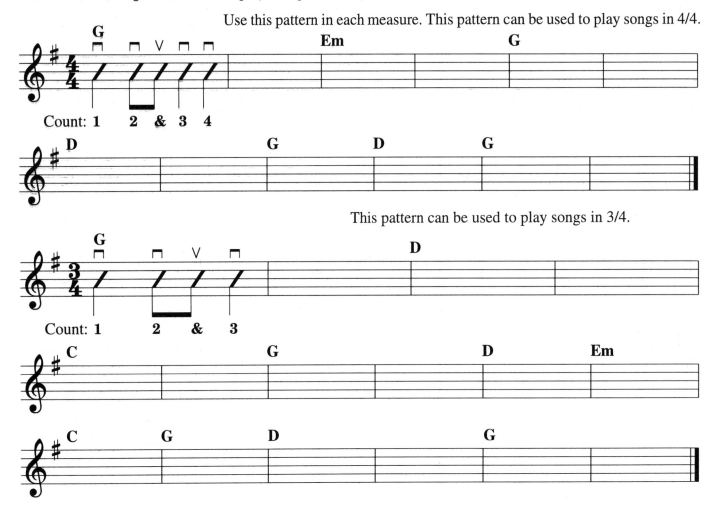

Practice the following song using the strum pattern written above the first measure.

Rollin' In My Sweet Baby's Arms

Basics

Am

D7

Learn the two new chords drawn here.

Practice the following exercises and songs which contain **Am** and **D7**.

Molly Malone

In Dub – lin's fair cit – y where girls are so pret – ty, oh,

there's where I met my sweet Mol – ly Ma – lone, And she

Wheeled her wheel – bar – row through the streets broad and nar – row cry – ing

"Cock – les and mus – sels, A – live, a – live – o." "A

live, a – live – o, _____ a – live, a – live – o" _____ Cry – ing

"Cock – les and mus – sels, A – live, a – live – o."

If two chords appear in a measure, you can strum each chord down two times:

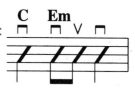

or divide the strum pattern in half:

If two chords appear in a measure in 3/4 time, strum the chord which gets the most space above the measure two times down, and the other chord down one time:

or strum the chord getting the most space down-up-down, and the other chord down one time:

Practice the following songs which contain some measures with two chords.

Midnight Special Blues

Unknown

Basics

Double Stops/Triads

When two or more notes are written on top of each other, play the notes at the same time. Figure out the placement of the notes, beginning with the top note.

Double Stop Study

MC

Greensleeves

CD #1 Track #24

MC
Trad. English Air

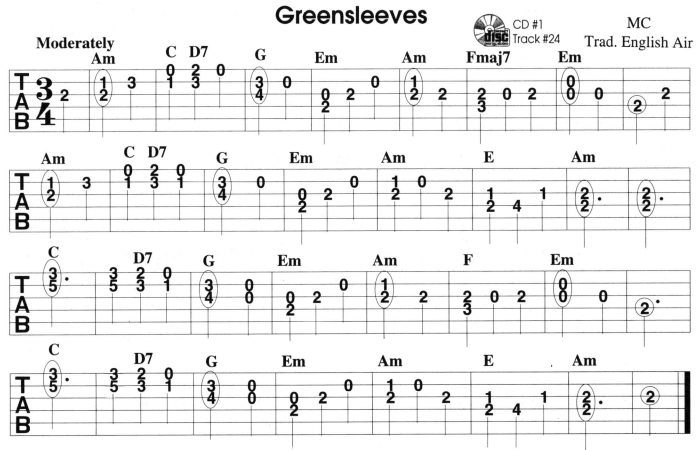

arr. © 1996 by Mel Bay Publications, Inc. All rights reserved.

Triads

WB

Minor Song

WB

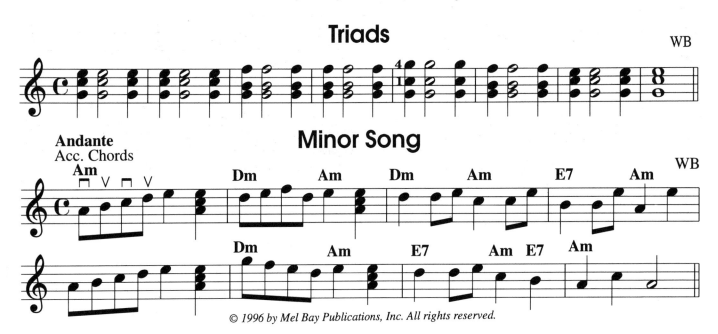

© 1996 by Mel Bay Publications, Inc. All rights reserved.

E Minor Pentatonic Scale

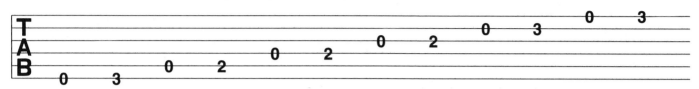

open strings

The diagram at right shows the E minor Pentatonic Scale. **Pentatonic** means this scale contains five notes within the octave. This scale can be used to improvise and create solos over the Em chord. It can also be played with blues in E and the E7 chord which will be discussed later in this book.

Practice playing the scale from the lowest note to the highest and then reverse the direction. Tablature for this scale is written under the diagram.

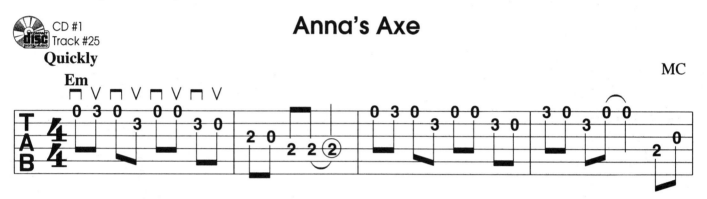

Practice playing the following solo which uses the **E minor pentatonic scale.**

CD #1
Track #25

Anna's Axe

Quickly

MC

Em

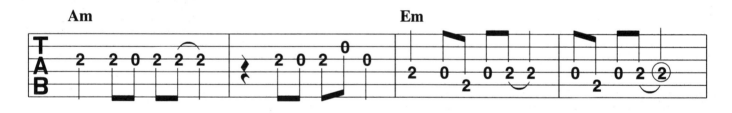

Am   Em

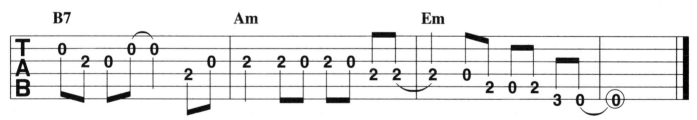

Moveable Pentatonic Scales

The following two diagrams show minor pentatonic scale patterns which can be moved up the neck. They will be used in later books of the *Mastering the Guitar* series.

Root →

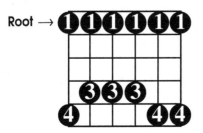

Root →

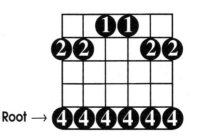

Basics

Notes on the Fourth String

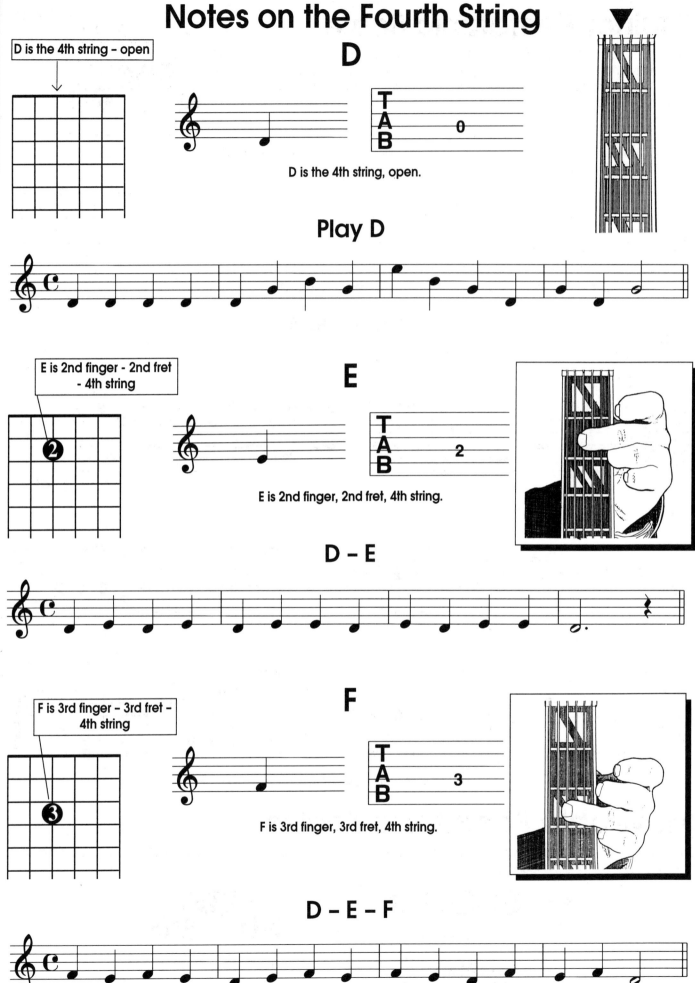

Basics

D

D is the 4th string – open

D is the 4th string, open.

Play D

E

E is 2nd finger - 2nd fret - 4th string

E is 2nd finger, 2nd fret, 4th string.

D – E

F

F is 3rd finger – 3rd fret – 4th string

F is 3rd finger, 3rd fret, 4th string.

D – E – F

Morning Song

CD #1
Track #26

Moderately
Acc. Chords

WB
Early American
Hymn Melody

Repeat Sign

Repeat signs look like this:

When they occur, repeat the music found between the signs.

Cripple Creek

CD #1
Track #27

Fast
Acc. Chords

WB
Western American
Gold Mining Song

Early Christmas Morn

CD #1
Track #28

Gently
Acc. Chords

WB
13th Century English

Basics

Solos

CD #1
Track #29

Spanish Nights

WB

Medium tempo
Acc. Chords

Four-String Blues

CD #1
Track #30

Easy walking tempo
Acc. Chords

WB

Irish Mist

CD #1
Track #31

WB

Bright

The Clock

Moderately
Acc. Chords

WB

Echoes

Smoothly
Acc. Chords

WB

Arpeggio Picking

Flowing
Acc. Chords

WB

Chimes

Medium, Gently
Acc. Chords

WB

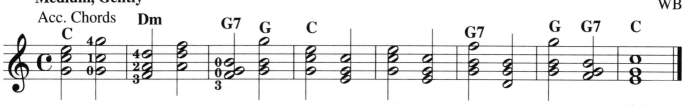

Basics

Tab Solos

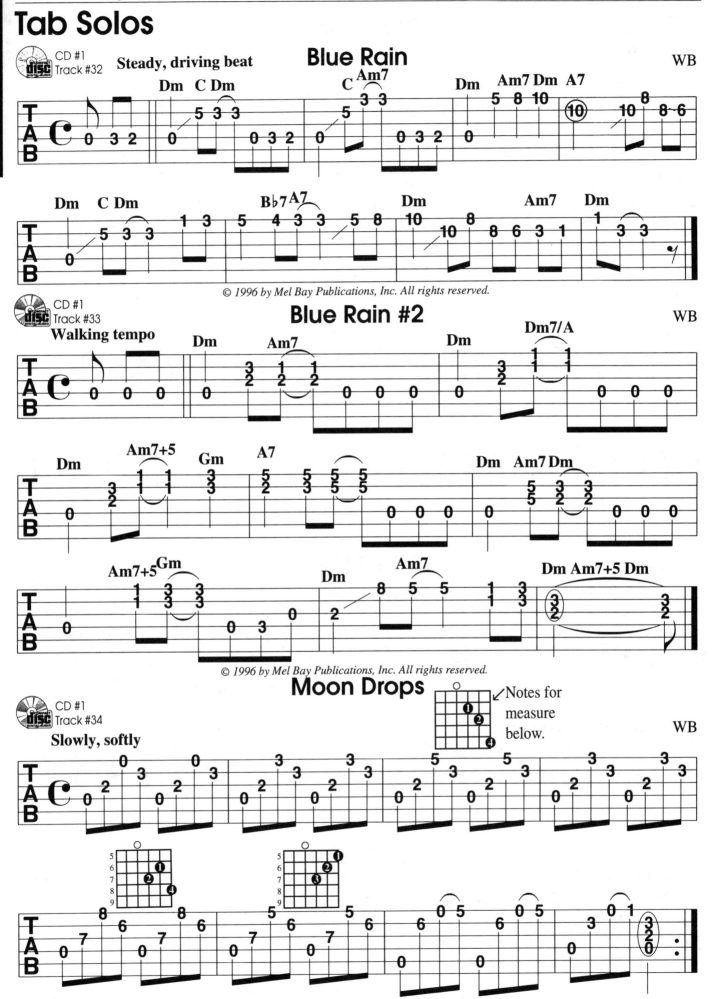

Notes on the 5th String

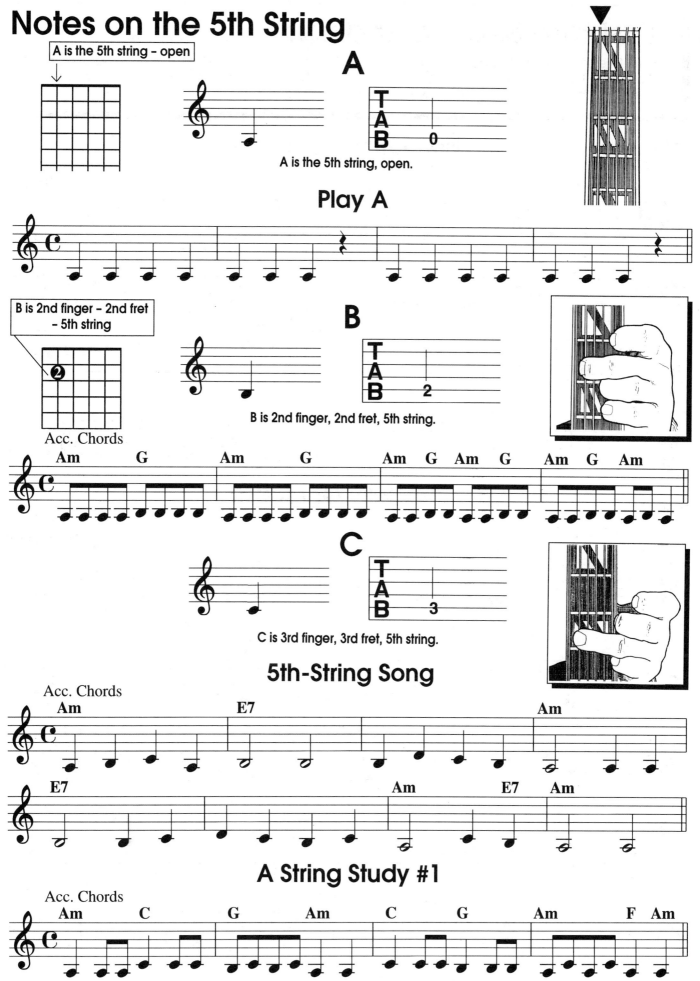

A is the 5th string - open

A

A is the 5th string, open.

Play A

B is 2nd finger – 2nd fret – 5th string

B

B is 2nd finger, 2nd fret, 5th string.

Acc. Chords

Am   G   Am   G   Am   G   Am   G   Am   G   Am

C

C is 3rd finger, 3rd fret, 5th string.

5th-String Song

Acc. Chords

Am   E7   Am

E7   Am   E7   Am

A String Study #1

Acc. Chords

Am   C   G   Am   C   G   Am   F   Am

First and Second Endings

Sometimes in a song a first and second ending appear. When this occurs, take the first ending and observe the repeat sign. Then, on the second time through, skip the first ending, play the second ending, and continue on with the music. (Sometimes the song will end with the second ending.)

CD #1
Track #35

Hungarian Dance #4

WB
Brahms

CD #1
Track #36

The Sally Gardens

WB
Irish Ballad

Dotted Quarter Note

A dotted quarter note receives one-and-a-half counts.

is the same as

Count: 1 & 2   1 & 2

Compare

1 & 2 & 1 & 2 & 1 & 2 & 1 & 2 &

Study

Dotted quarter note

Count: 1 & 2 & 3 & 4 &

Misty Morn

Moderately
Acc. Chords

CD #1 Track #37

WB

Call the Ewes

Slowly
Acc. Chords

CD #1 Track #38

WB
Scottish Ballad

Cumberland Ridge

CD #1 Track #39

WB

Tab Solos

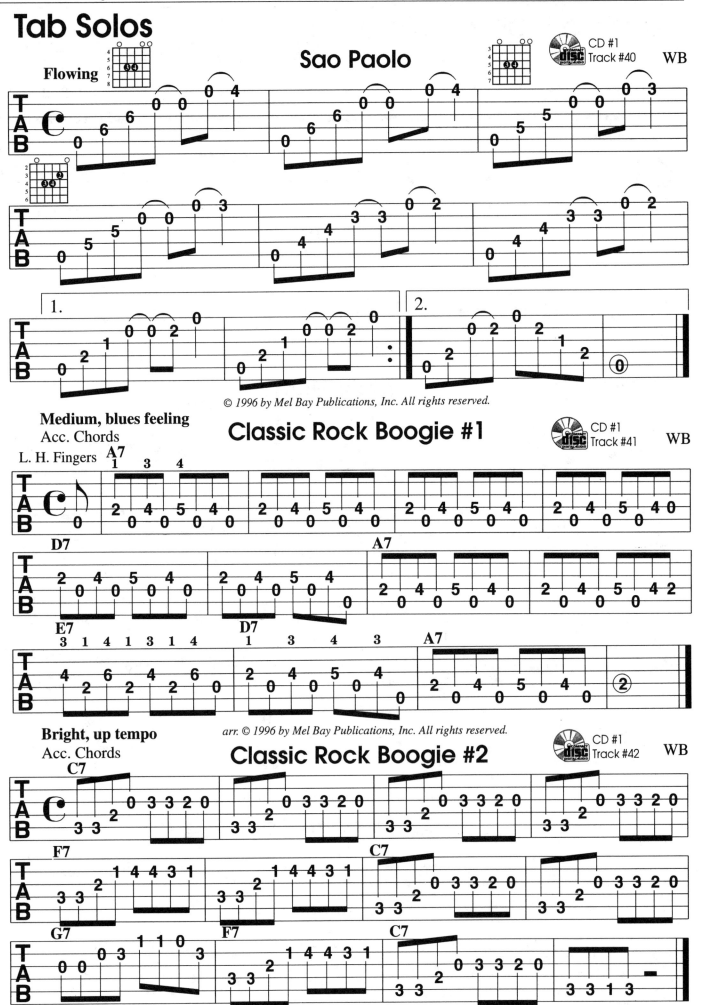

Sao Paolo

Flowing

CD #1 Track #40   WB

© 1996 by Mel Bay Publications, Inc. All rights reserved.

Medium, blues feeling
Acc. Chords
L. H. Fingers

Classic Rock Boogie #1

CD #1 Track #41   WB

arr. © 1996 by Mel Bay Publications, Inc. All rights reserved.

Bright, up tempo
Acc. Chords

Classic Rock Boogie #2

CD #1 Track #42   WB

arr. © 1996 by Mel Bay Publications, Inc. All rights reserved.

Notes on the 6th String

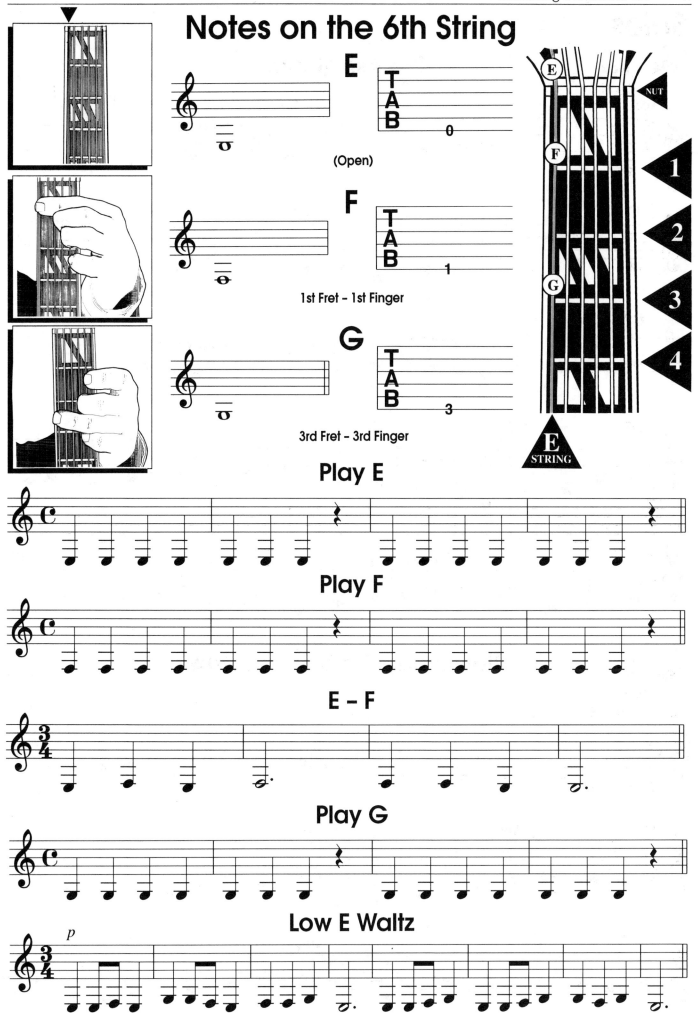

E

(Open)

F

1st Fret – 1st Finger

G

3rd Fret – 3rd Finger

Play E

Play F

E – F

Play G

Low E Waltz

Basics

Solos

CD #1
Track #43

The Ash Grove

WB
English Folk Melody

Moderately
Acc. Chords **C**

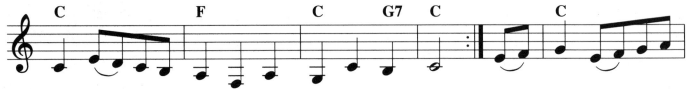

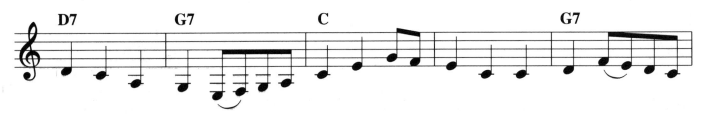

CD #1
Track #44

Blow Away the Morning Dew

WB
Sea Chanty

Brightly
Acc. Chords **C**

Block Chords

When more than three notes are played together, the chord that results is called a **block chord.** Block chords can contain four, five, or six notes. As with triads play the notes quickly so they sound at the same time.

Practice the following pieces which contain **triads** and **block chords.**

Black Is the Color of My True Love's Hair

CD #1
Track #45

MC

Spanish Romance

CD #1
Track #46

MC

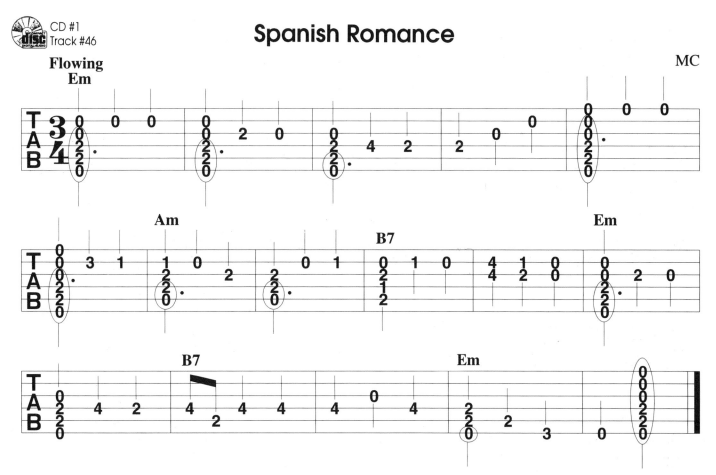

CD #1
Track #47

O mio babbino caro

MC
Puccini

Slowly, smoothly

Play the G note
fourth string, fifth fret.

The C Scale

C Scale

Extended C Scale

C Picking Study #1

C Picking Study #2

C Velocity Study #1

C Velocity Study #2

Key of C

C Velocity Study #3

WB

C Velocity Study #4

WB

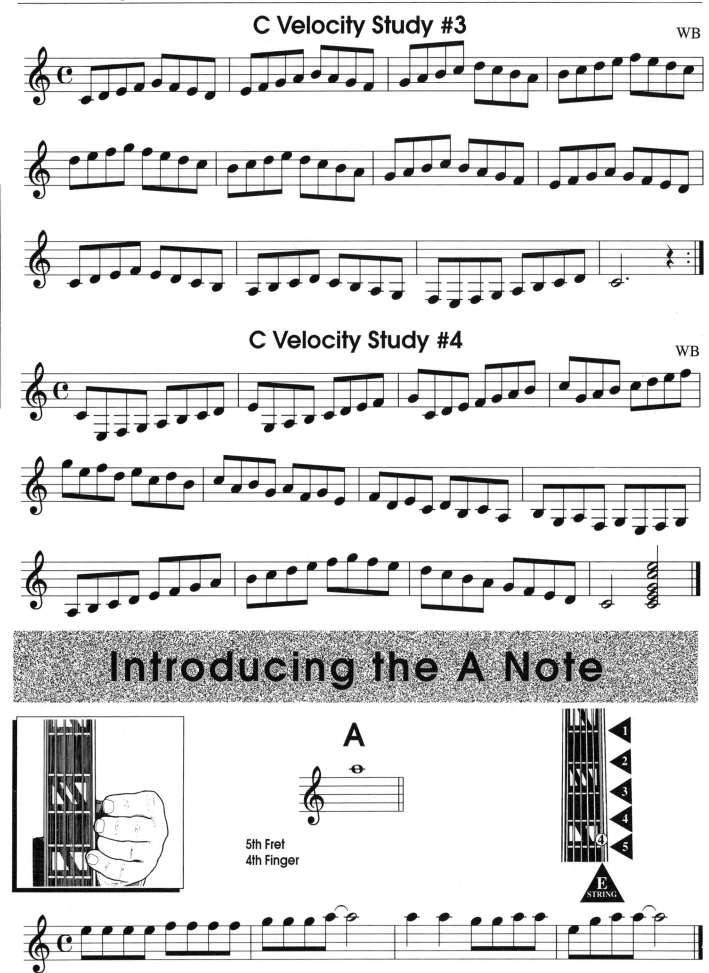

Introducing the A Note

A

5th Fret
4th Finger

E
STRING

You are now ready to begin working through the supplementary guitar studies in the *Mastering the Guitar: Technique Studies* book.

Solos

Blow, Ye Winds

CD #1 Track #48

Brightly
Acc. Chords

WB
Sea Chanty

Early American Hymn

CD #1 Track #49

Slowly
Acc. Chords

WB

Bass Line Lead/Bluegrass Style

CD #1 Track #50

Swing feeling
Acc. Chords

WB

Key of C

Cruisin' Sunset

CD #1
Track #51

MC

Moderately, let notes ring

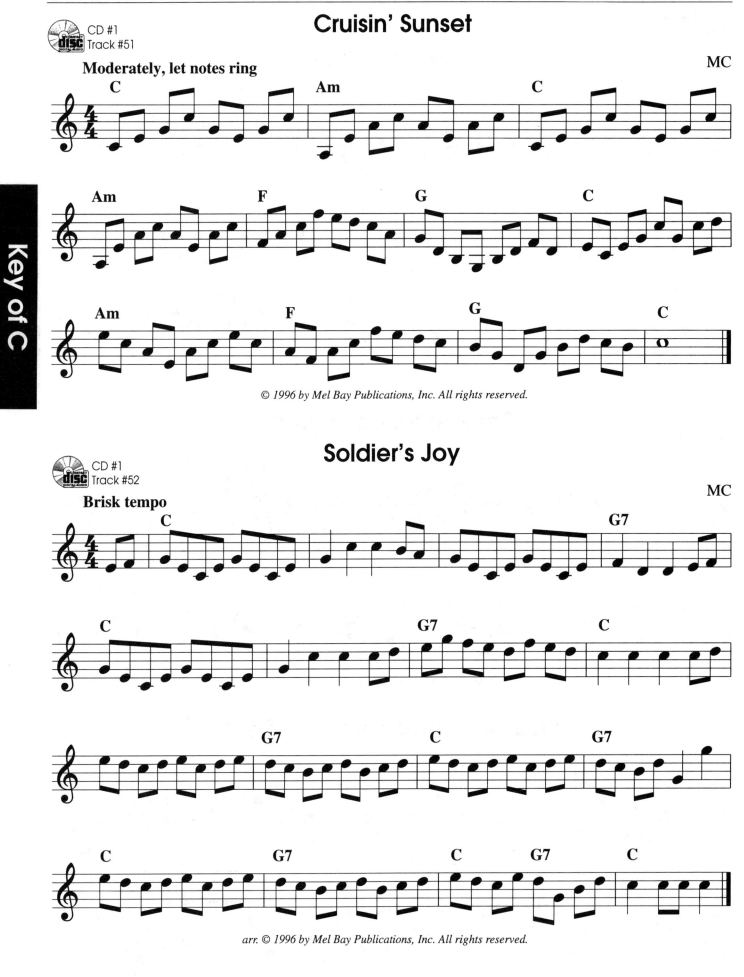

Soldier's Joy

CD #1
Track #52

MC

Brisk tempo

Key of C

Flyin' South

CD #1
Track #53

MC

Bright tempo

Key of C

Danny Boy

CD #1
Track #54

MC
Irish Ballad

Slowly

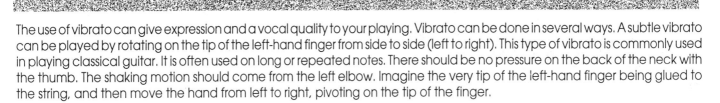

Vibrato

The use of vibrato can give expression and a vocal quality to your playing. Vibrato can be done in several ways. A subtle vibrato can be played by rotating on the tip of the left-hand finger from side to side (left to right). This type of vibrato is commonly used in playing classical guitar. It is often used on long or repeated notes. There should be no pressure on the back of the neck with the thumb. The shaking motion should come from the left elbow. Imagine the very tip of the left-hand finger being glued to the string, and then move the hand from left to right, pivoting on the tip of the finger.

Practice playing the following long and repeated notes using this type of vibrato.

Play the next solo using vibrato on the long and repeated notes.

Spanish Knights

MC

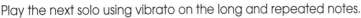

The type of vibrato which is commonly used in the blues is done by quickly bending and releasing the string with the left hand. The left hand should touch the neck at the base of the first finger and the hand should pivot back and forth. The string is bent by turning the left-hand wrist and forearm rather than pulling with the left-hand finger. Illustration no. 1 shows the position of the left hand. Illustration no. 2 shows the left hand pivoting and bending the string. The *rocking* of the left hand between the positions is illustration no. 1, and the position in illustration no. 2 causes the vibrato.

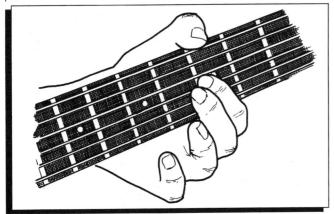

Blues vibrato illustration no. 1

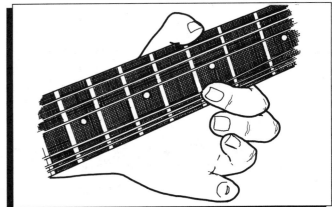

Blues vibrato illustration no. 2

Vibrato is indicated with a wavy line written above the note (～～). Even if the vibrato is not indicated, vibrato can be used on long and repeated notes.

Practice the following exercise using vibrato.

Vibrato Study

Vibrato Study #2

Bending the Blues

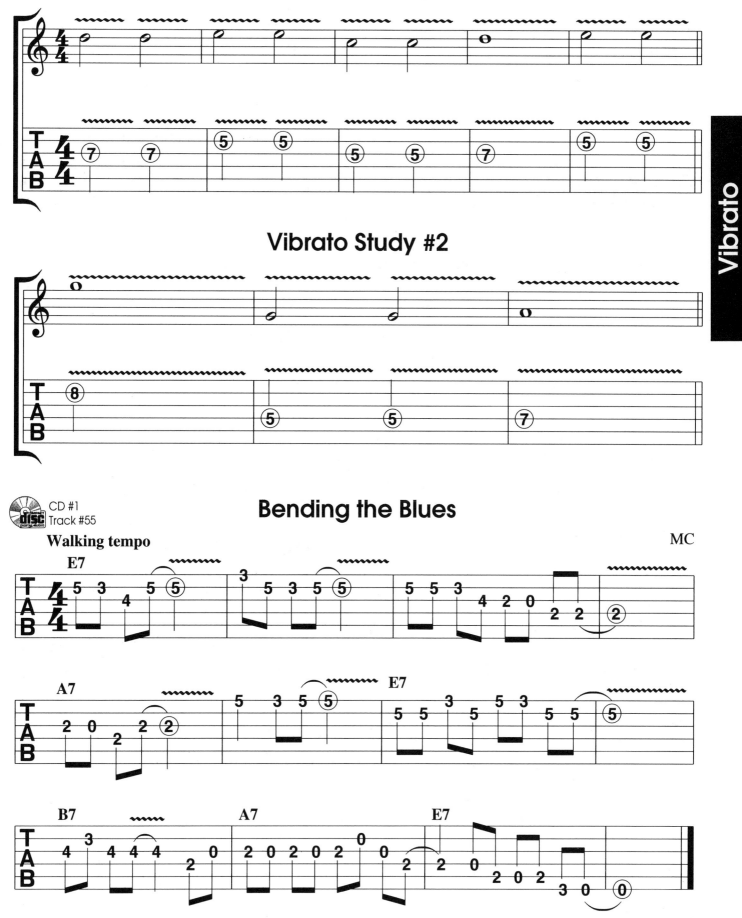

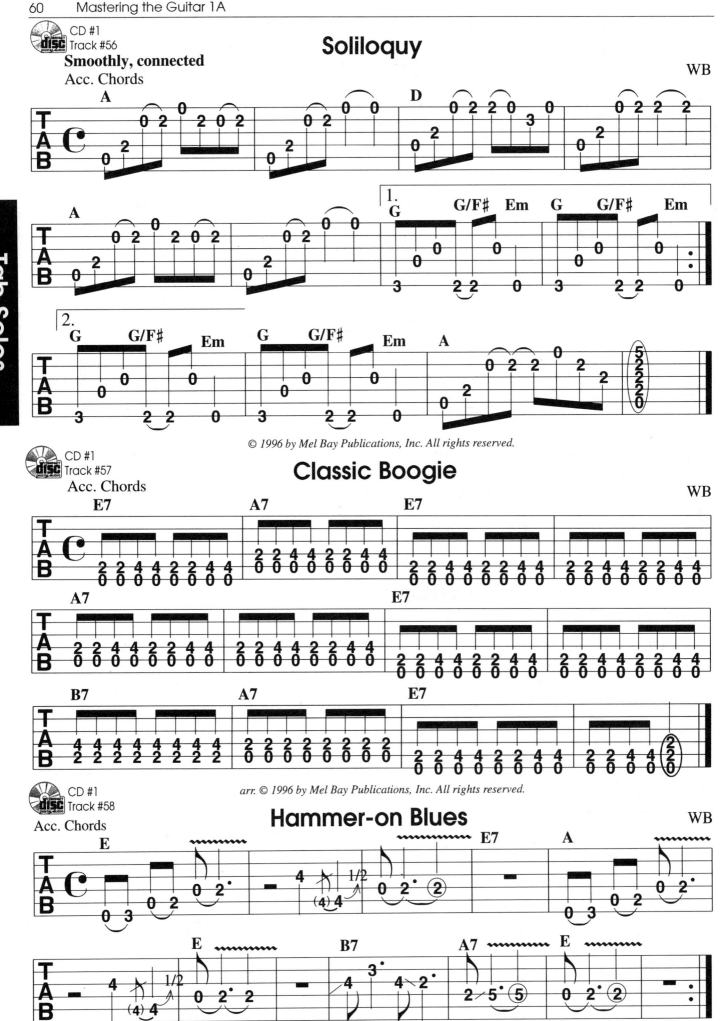

Rock/Blues Solos Utilizing Lower Strings

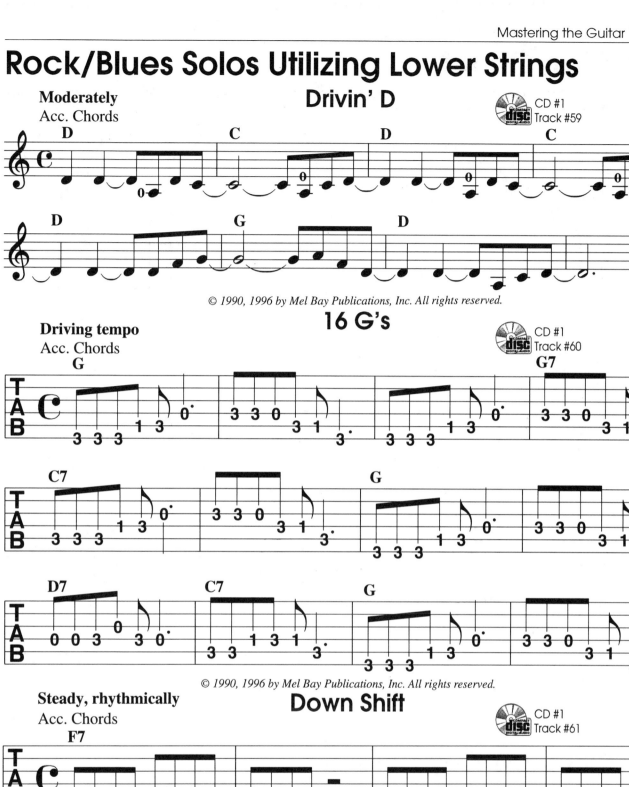

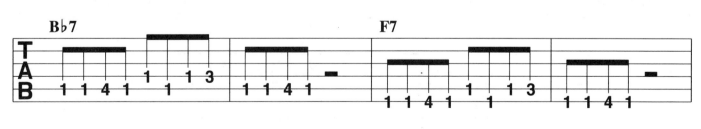

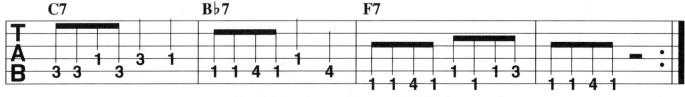

Lower String Solos

F and Dm Chords

Drawn below are the **F** and **Dm** chords. Learn these chords and practice the exercises which are written below the diagrams. This indicates the left hand. First finger lays (bars) across two strings.

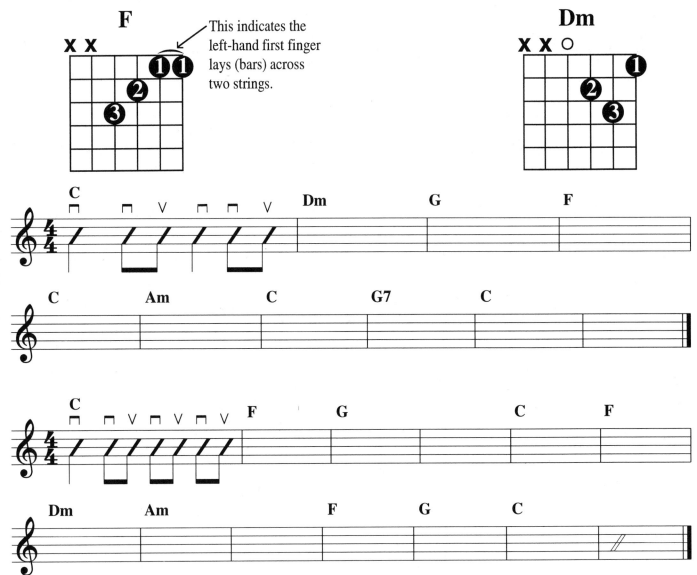

This indicates the left-hand first finger lays (bars) across two strings.

Chords in the Key of C

The chords in the key of C are: C, Dm, Em, F, G, and Am. Notice the chords in the key are given in alphabetical order. Each of the chords in this key is built upon six steps of the C major scale. It's helpful in memorizing the chords in each key, if they are placed alphabetically. On the chart below, the chords in the key of C are listed in scale order, and each chord has been assigned a Roman numeral. The Roman numeral assigned to the chord corresponds to the step of the C major scale which has the same letter name as the chord.

Six Basic Chords in the Key of C					
C	Dm	Em	F	G(7)	Am
I	ii	iii	IV	V	vi

Notice the major chords are assigned large Roman numerals and the minor chords are assigned small Roman numerals. When the chords in any key are placed in alphabetical order the I, IV, and V chords will be major and ii, iii, and vi chords will be minor. As in the key of C, for the other keys, the chords will have the same letter names as the first six steps of the major scale for that key. Notice that the V chord (in the key of C, the G chord) can be major or a seventh chord.

Chords in C

Knowing the Roman numerals assigned to the chords in a key will be very helpful later in transposing (changing the key), and learning elements of music theory.

The following exercises are in the **key of C.** Notice that the Roman numeral assigned to the chord for the key of C is written in parenthesis next to the chord name.

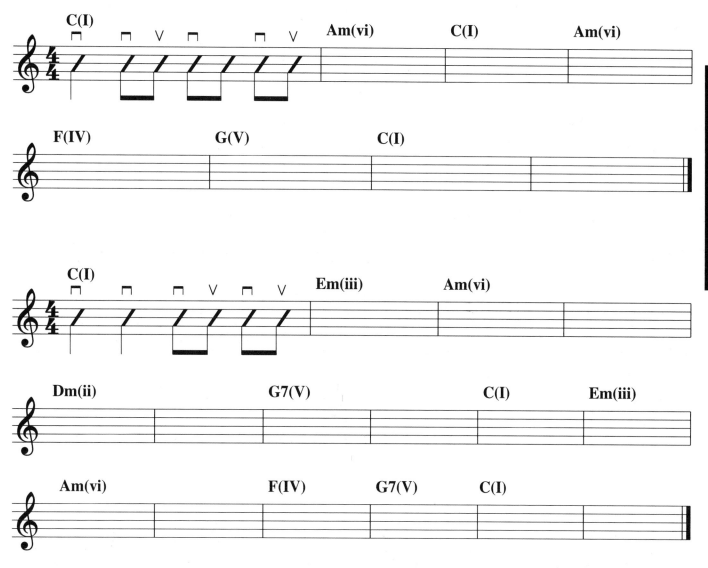

Common Chord Progressions

Written on the next page are some very popular and common chord progressions. As the chords in other keys are present in this book, they can be "plugged-in" to the Roman numerals in these exercises, and the same exercise can be played in a different key. The chords for the key of C have been written in parenthesis next to the Roman numerals. Strum each exercise. Notice that the exercises may be played in 4/4 or 3/4. Use any of the strum patterns for 4/4 or 3/4 which have been used up to now in this book. After you select a pattern, use the same strum pattern in each measure.

Common Chord Progressions

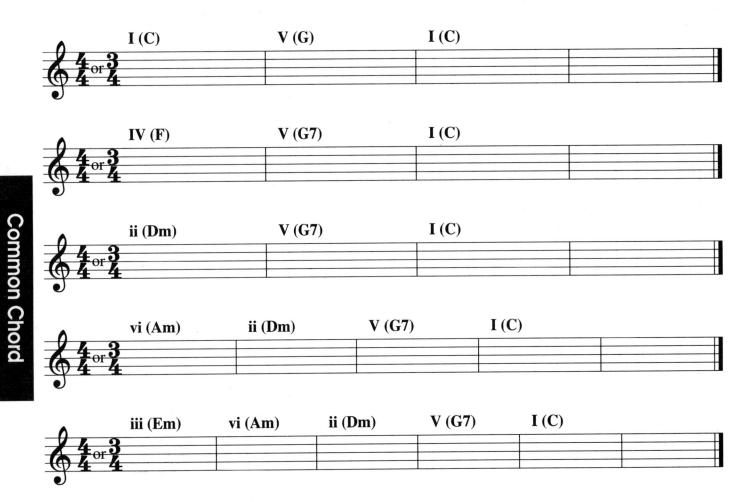

Practice playing the chords to the next song, which is in the **key of C** and uses chords from the key of C.

Man of Constant Sorrow

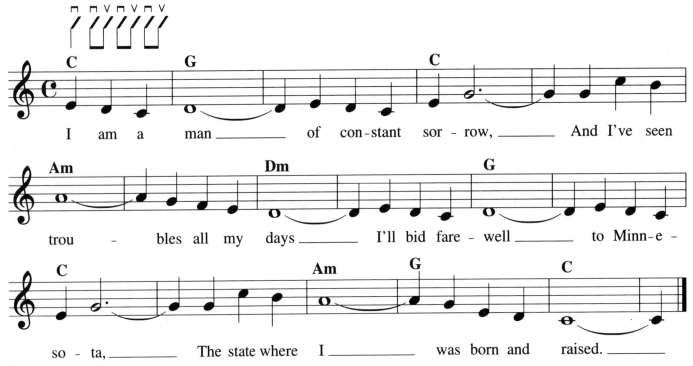

Sharps

A "**sharp**" placed in front of a note *raises* the pitch ½ step or 1 fret. Study the notes below. We will learn more about sharps as we learn specific keys later on.

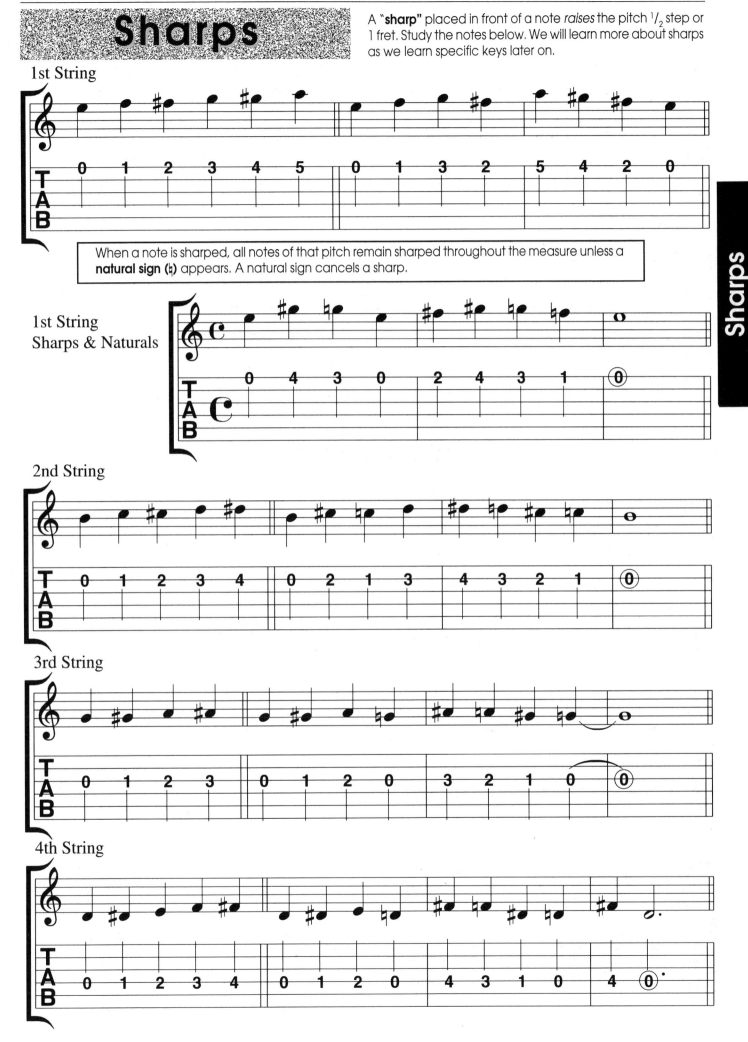

When a note is sharped, all notes of that pitch remain sharped throughout the measure unless a **natural sign** (♮) appears. A natural sign cancels a sharp.

5th String

6th String

Walking Guitar

WB

D.C. al Fine

When this phrase appears at the end of a piece **(D.C. al Fine)** go back to the beginning and play until you see the word **"Fine,"** which means "The End."

Acres of Bluegrass

CD #1 Track #62   MC

Solos with Sharps

Xiomara

Play the following solo containing the eighth rest.

CD #1 Track #63   MC

A7 and E7 Chords

The fingerings for **A7** and **E7** chords are shown on the diagrams below. Notice there are two fingerings for each chord. One is not necessarily better than the other and either fingering may be used. The first forms are easier. Eventually, both forms of each chord should be learned.

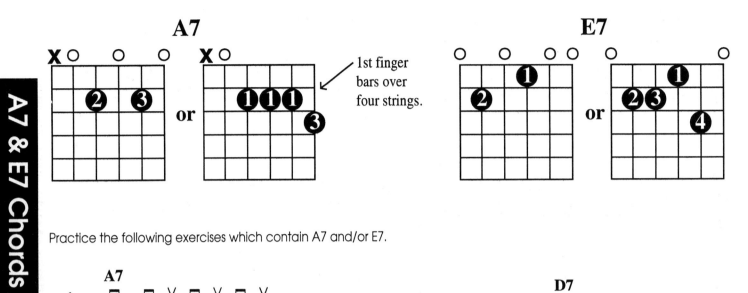

Practice the following exercises which contain A7 and/or E7.

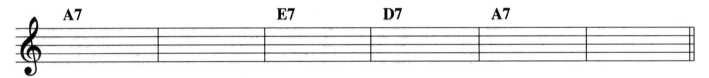

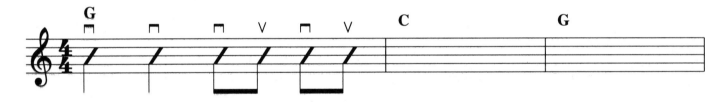

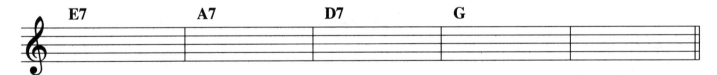

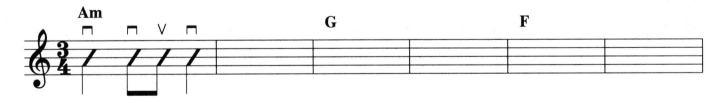

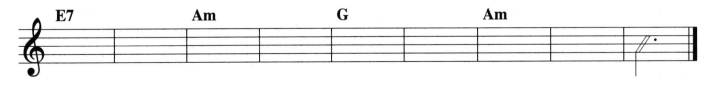

B7 and Bm Chords

Learn the **B7** and **Bm** chords drawn below and practice the exercises containing these chords. As with the other exercises in this book, use the same strum pattern which is written in the first measure to play the other measures.

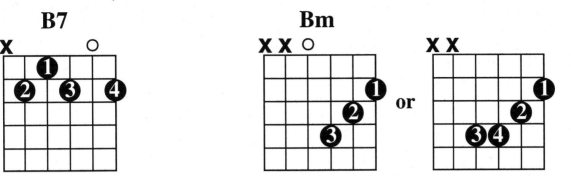

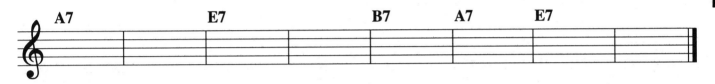

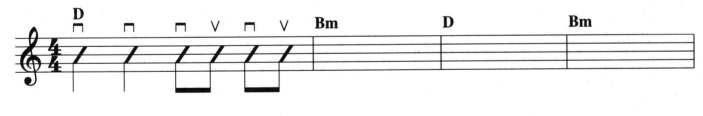

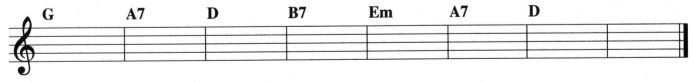

Syncopation

Syncopation means placing the accent on a beat (or a part of the beat) which is normally weak. Syncopation is often done by playing a note on the up beat (second half of the beat, or the "and") and letting that note ring through the first half of the next beat. Syncopated rhythms are commonly written as a quarter note or quarter notes between two eighth notes. Sometimes the second eighth note is replaced by a dot after the quarter note. The following illustrations show how syncopated rhythms are written and how they are counted. Some of the songs, exercises, and solos in this book contain these rhythms. It's important that you understand how they are counted. Hold any note and practice tapping your foot on the beat while you play and count aloud the rhythms written below.

Practice the following exercises and song which contain **syncopation**.

CD #1
Track #64

Spanish Groove

Moderately

MC

Syncopated Strums

Shown below are common strum patterns for 4/4 and 3/4 which contain syncopation. They can be used to play the chords to any song in 4/4 or 3/4. Each pattern takes one measure to complete. Hold any chord and practice each pattern. Count aloud as you play the patterns. Be sure to wait for the tied strums.

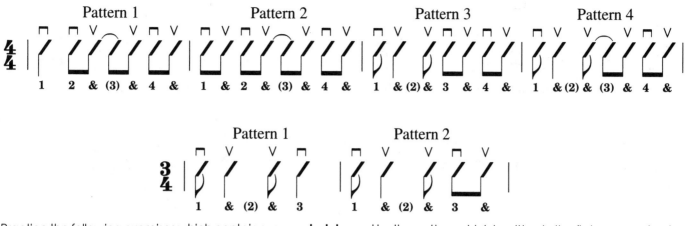

Practice the following exercises which contain **syncopated strums.** Use the pattern which is written in the first measure to play each measure of the exercise.

Practice the following song which uses a syncopated strum.

Oh, Sinner Man

1. Oh, sin - ner man _____ where you gon - na run to; Oh, sin - ner

man _____ where you gon - na run to? Oh, sin - ner man _____

where you gon - na run to, all _____ on that day? _____

Strum Patterns Review

Shown below are the strum patterns which have been used in this book so far. These patterns can be used to play songs in 4/4 or 3/4. Each pattern takes one measure to complete. The patterns are listed in order of difficulty. Hold any chord and review these patterns, then apply them to songs from this book, songbooks, and sheet music.

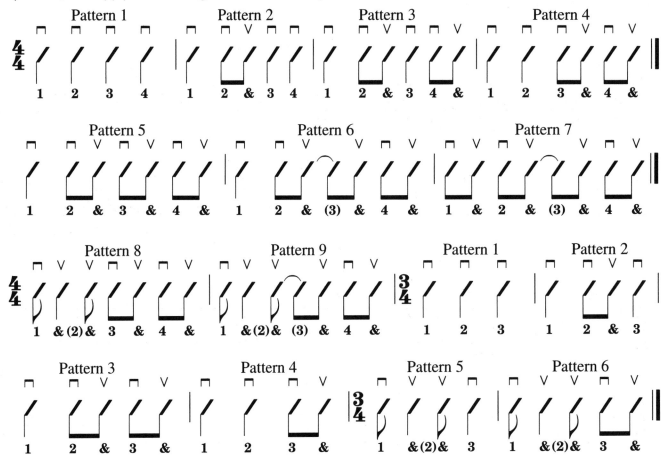

Strums (vertical tab on left margin)

The Blues Progression

One of the most popular forms of the blues is the 12-bar blues progression. The term **progression** refers to a series of chords. **Twelve-bar** means the progression is 12 measures long. *The three chords used in the basic 12-bar progression are the I, IV, and V chords.* The **I chord** (sometimes called the **tonic**) has the same letter name as the key in which you are playing. For example, the I chord in the key of C is C. The **IV chord (subdominant)** has the letter name which is four steps up the major scale from the I chord. The IV chord in the key of C is F. The **V chord (dominant)** has the same letter name as the fifth step up the major scale from the I chord. The V chord in the key of C is G. The following chart shows the I, IV, and V chords in the different keys. The most common keys are shown first.

Key ↓

I (Tonic)	IV (Subdominant)	V (Dominant)
E	A	B
A	D	E
D	G	A
G	C	D
C	F	G
F	B♭	C
B♭	E♭	F
E♭	A♭	B♭
A♭	D♭	E♭
D♭	G♭	A♭
B	E	F♯
F♯	B	C♯
G♭	C♭	D♭

Blues

The formula for building the basic 12-bar blues progression is: four measures of the I chord, two measures of the IV chord, two measures of the I chord, one measure of the V chord, one measure of the IV chord, and two measures of the I chord. It's very common to replace the last measure of the I chord with a V chord if the progression is going to be repeated. This last measure is sometimes called the ***turnaround.*** The advantage of knowing the Roman numeral formula is that, by plugging in the correct I, IV, and V chords, you can play the blues in any key.

The following exercise is the basic 12-bar blues progression. Notice that the number of measures that each chord is played fits the blues formula. The chords in parentheses are the chords which would be used to play the blues in the key of E. Seventh chords (7) are commonly used on every chord in the blues because of their dissonant quality.

Play the following progression strumming down four times in each measure. While it may seem overly simple, strumming down four times in a measure was, and is, a fairly popular technique. Accent beats two and four.

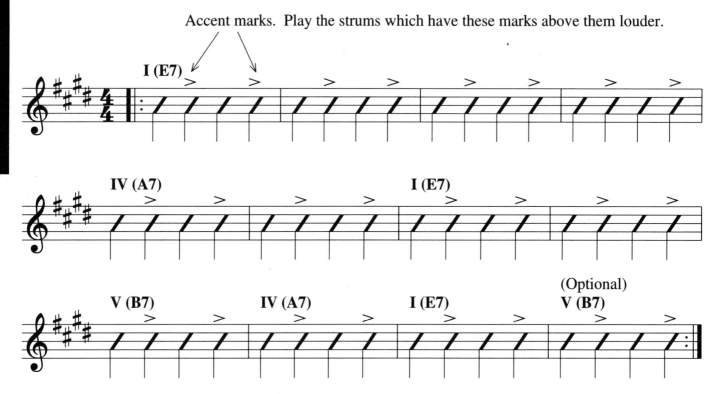

Accent marks. Play the strums which have these marks above them louder.

The next progression is a very **common variation of the 12-bar blues.** *The IV chord has been added in the second measure.* Remember the V chord in the last measure is optional. This chord can be played if the progression is going to be repeated. If you're not repeating the progression, play the I chord in the last measure. Practice strumming this exercise. In each measure of the progression, play the strum pattern which is written in the first measure. This strum pattern works well when playing songs in 4/4.

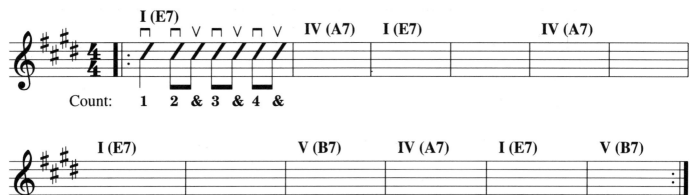

Strum the next progression which is a **blues in the key of A.** In each measure, use the strum pattern which is written in the first measure. This is another strum pattern which works to accompany songs in 4/4.

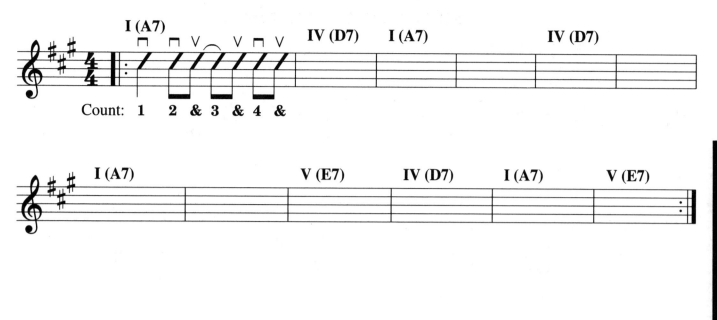

Count: 1   2 & 3 & 4 &

To play the blues in a minor key, the i and iv chords are minor and the V chord is still a seventh chord. Small Roman numerals indicate minor chords. Practice strumming the following blues in A minor. Use any of the strum patterns for 4/4. Remember to use the same strum pattern in each measure.

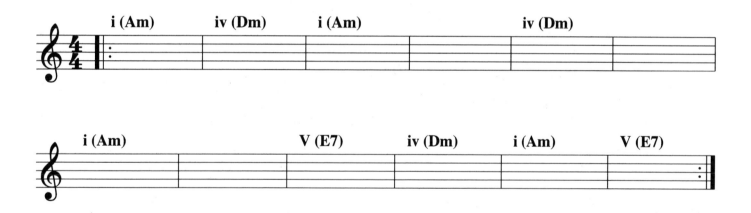

Blues

Practice strumming the following **blues songs.** Notice each song uses the 12-bar blues progression.

Baby Don't Love Me

MC

I love my baby,___ but my ba-by don't love_ me

I love my baby,___ but my ba-by don't love_ me.

Feelin' down and lonely._ Wish these blues would set me ___ free. _

You're the Cure

MC

Help a sick man baby.____ Won't you help me please?

Help a sick man baby._ Won't you help_ me please?

All I need's your lovin'._ You're the cure for my dis - ease.

Power Chords

The type of chord which is commonly used in rock and blues guitar playing is called a **power chord.** Power chords are written with the 5 next to the chord name (A5). Power chords may also be used when the written chord is a seventh (7) chord. The following diagrams show the A5, D5, and E5 chords. Only two strings are played on each chord. One of the strings played is open. Play the strings quickly so they sound simultaneously. The tablature and notes which are played are written next to each diagram. Hold each chord and play it several times.

A5

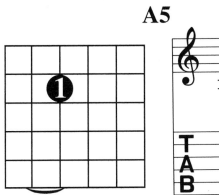 

Play strings five and four.

D5

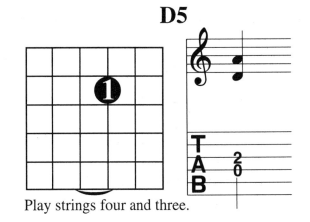

Play strings four and three.

E5

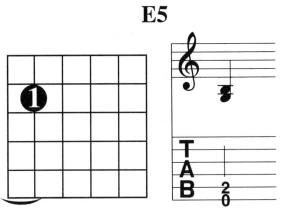

Play strings six and five.

A popular way of using power chords for the guitar accompaniment is to play each chord eight times in a measure (two times to each beat). Play the next blues progression which shows how this is done. The eighth note strums are written as two strum bars connected with a beam (   ). This shows that the chord is played two times to each beat (once on the downbeat and once in between the beats). Notice that only downstrokes are used. Be sure to play only two strings on each power chord.

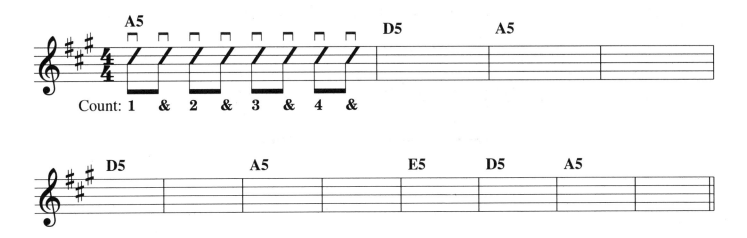

Count: 1   &   2   &   3   &   4   &

It is very common to play eighth notes (two notes or strums to a beat) to use **shuffle** or **swing** rhythm. This means that, rather than dividing the beat into two equal parts, the beat is divided into a long–short pattern. The eighth notes will sound more like a one-beat triplet with the middle note tied (♫ = ♩♪). This gives the music a kind of bouncy feel.

Practice the last exercise again using swing (or shuffle) rhythm.

A common variation on the power chord involves adding a finger on the third, fourth, seventh, and eighth downstrokes of the measure. For example, on the A5 chord, play strings 5 and 4 together four times. Use only downstrokes. On the third and fourth strokes, add the left-hand third finger where the "X" is drawn on the diagram below. Do this twice in each measure. Be sure to leave the first finger down even when the third finger is added.

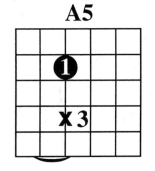

Add the third finger on these stroke

$$\frac{4}{4}$$

Count: 1   &   2   &   3   &   4   &

The following shows the notation and tablature for this technique.

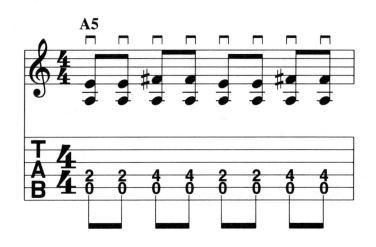

This technique could be used on the D5 chord by adding the third finger on the third string where the "X" is drawn.

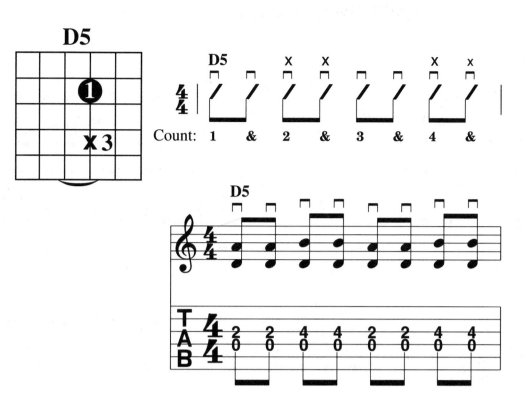

For the E5, add the third finger in the fourth fret on the fifth string.

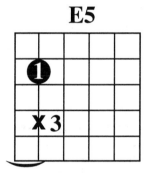

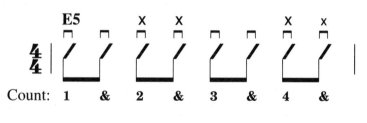

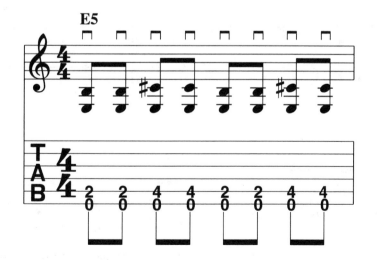

The next exercise uses this **variation on the power chords.**

CD #1
Track #65

Smithfield Boogie

MC

Moderately

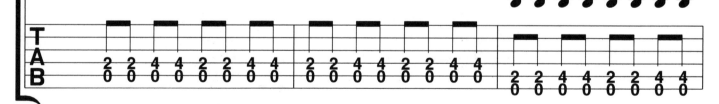

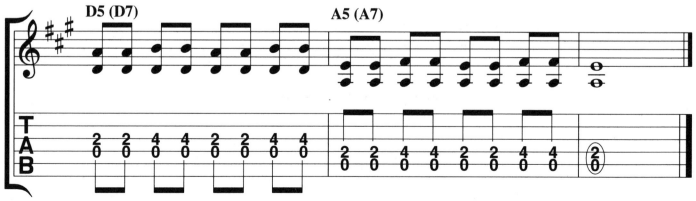

Power Chords

Another popular variation on power chords is to add the left-hand third finger on the third and seventh downstrokes of the measure (beats two and four). In the next song, the guitar accompaniment uses this variation on the power chords. The melody is written on the top staff and the guitar part is written below. Remember, power chords can be used if the written chord is a seventh (7) chord.

CD #1
Track #66

Good Mornin' Blues

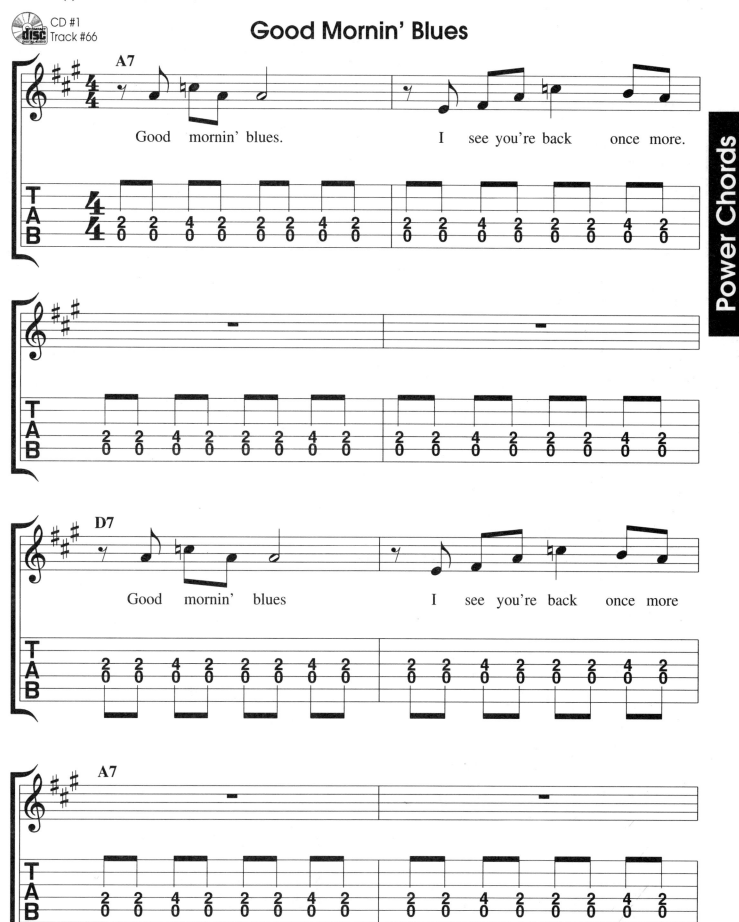

Good mornin' blues.   I see you're back   once more.

Good mornin' blues   I see you're back   once more

Power Chords

Power Chords

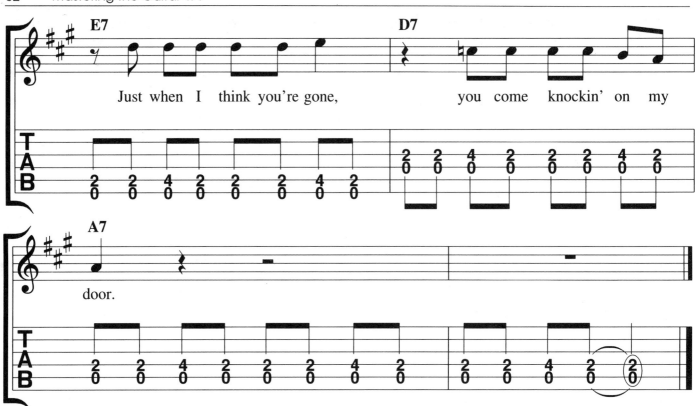

Just when I think you're gone,   you come knockin' on my

door.

Still another variation on the power chord involves adding another note to the basic power chord. In the diagrams below, the "X" shows where the first variation to the power chord was located. The circle shows where another note can be added to the power chord. It is common to use the left hand, third finger to add this note. The notation and tablature below the diagrams show how this new variation would be played.

A5

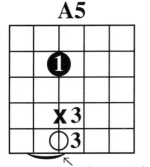

Play only strings five and four

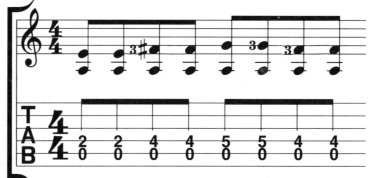

D5

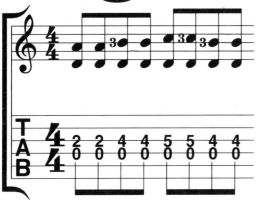

E5

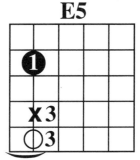

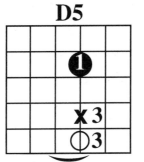

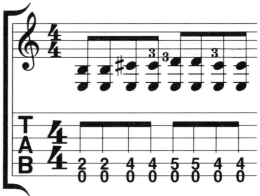

Play the following exercise which shows the power chord variation.

Midnight Drive

CD #1
Track #67

MC

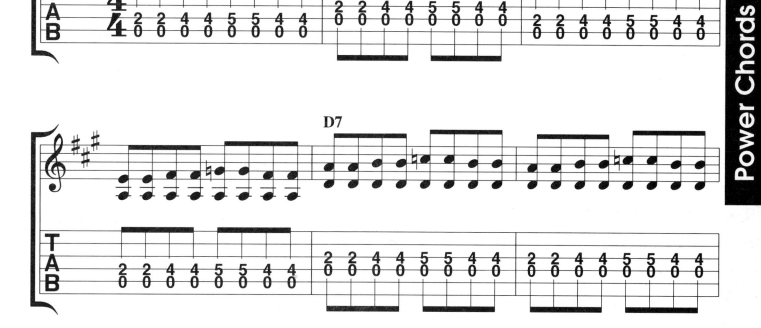

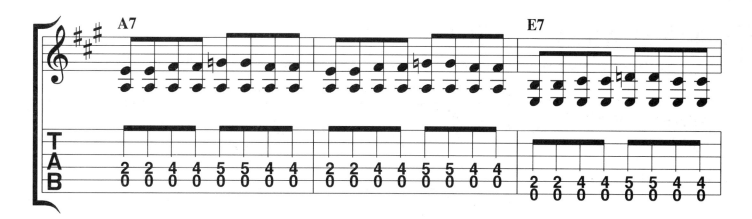

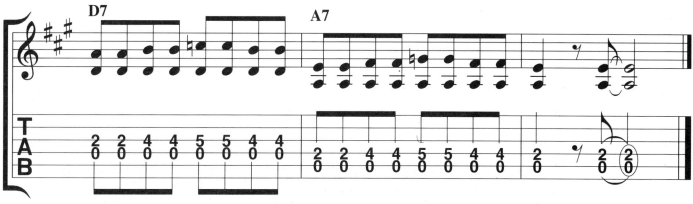

Power Chords

Key of A minor

The Natural A Minor Scale

You will notice that, like the C scale, there are no sharps or flats.

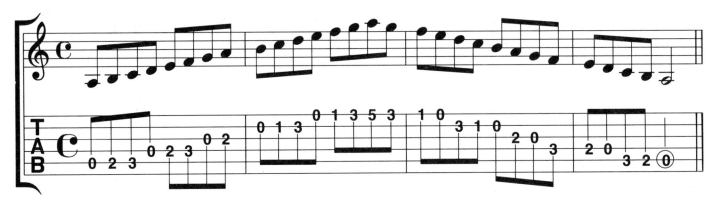

Velocity Study

A Harmonic Minor

In a harmonic minor scale the 7th tone of the scale is sharped. Thus with the "A" Harmonic Minor, all G's are played as G♯.

Velocity Study

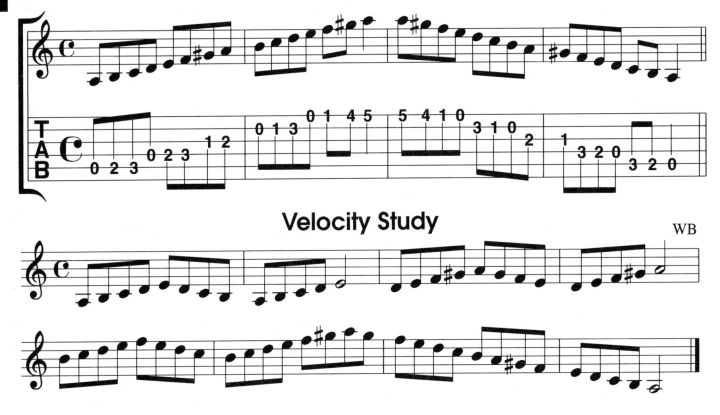

God Rest Ye Merry Gentlemen

Na Pali Coast

Key of A Minor

CD #1
Track #70

Sakura

MC

Key of A Minor

CD #1
Track #71

Minuet

WB
Henry Purcell

D.S. al (𝄋) Fine

When this phrase appears at the end of a piece (**D.S. 𝄋 al Fine**) go back to the sign (𝄋) and play until you see the word **"Fine,"** which means "The End."

Menuet

CD #1
Track #72

Acc. Chords

WB
Johann Quantz

Caleb's Gorge

CD #1 Track #73

WB

Parson's Farewell

CD #1 Track #74

WB
English Country Dance
By John Playford 1651

Key of A Minor

Eleven Mile Canyon

CD #1
Track #75

WB

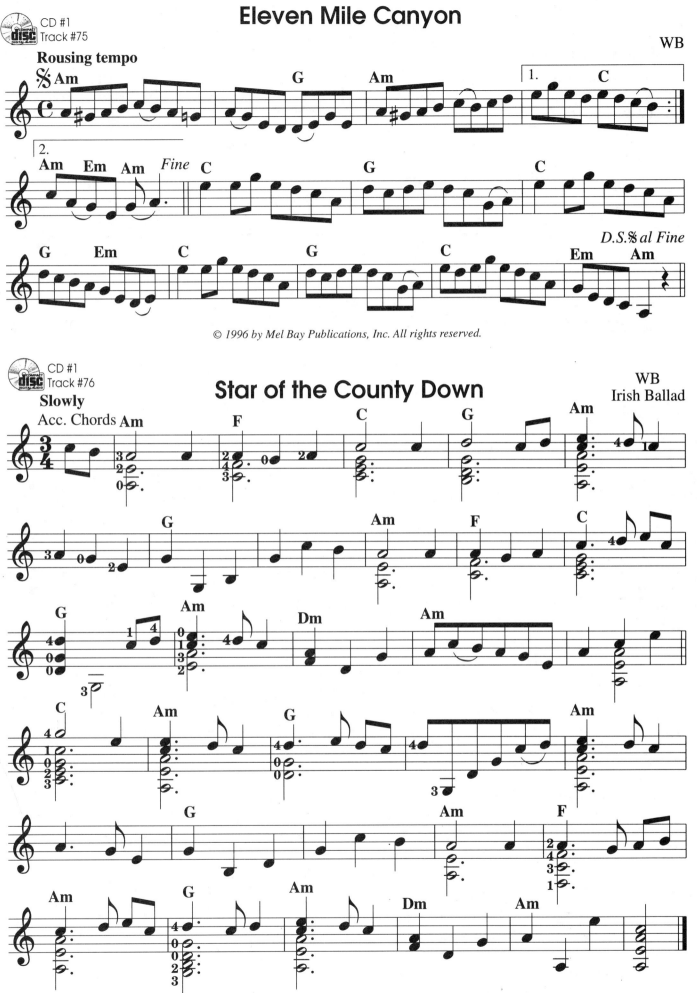

CD #1
Track #76

Star of the County Down

WB
Irish Ballad

Key of A Minor

Triplets

A **triplet** is a group of three notes played in the time of two notes of the same kind.

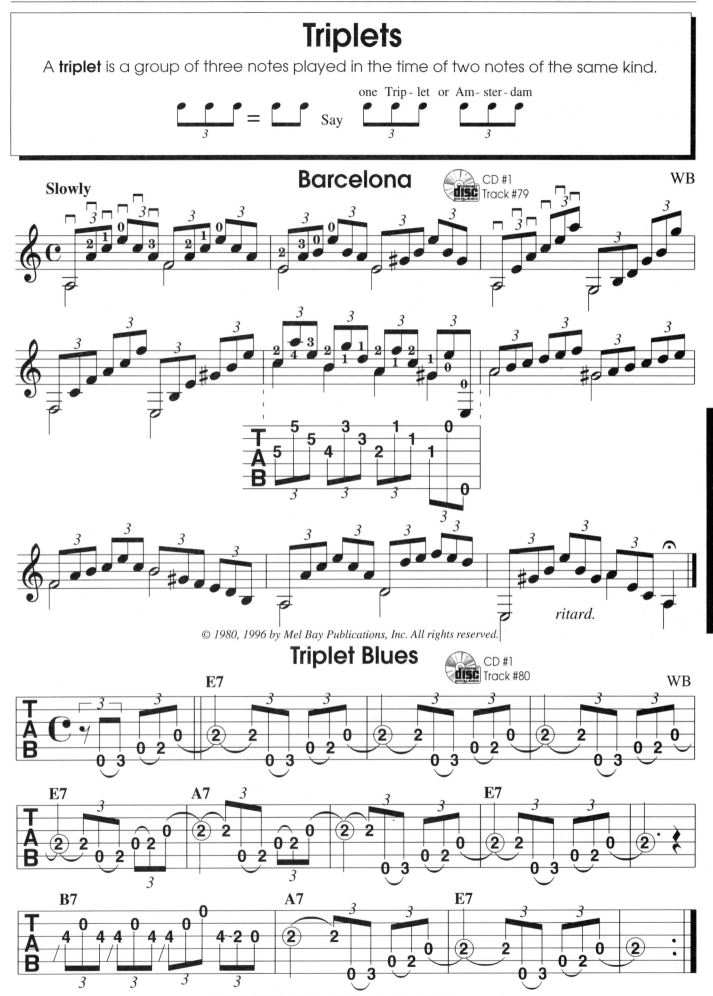

Jimmy's Shuffle

MC

Moderate, driving

Shady Grove

WB
Southern Mountain Song

Moderately
Acc. Chords

Key of A Minor

Two-Beat (Quarter Note) Triplets

When three quarter notes have a bracket and a number three under, or above them, this is a quarter note (or a two-beat) triplet.

These three notes are to be played in two beats. The two beats are divided into three equal parts. The two-beat triplet can be counted "tri-pel-et" or it may help to say "cho-co-late."

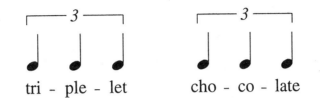

Usually, the notes in a two-beat triplet are picked down–down–down.

Practice the following exercise and solo which contain two-beat triplets.

Not Forgetting Her

CD #2 Track #1

MC

Moderately slow

Key of A Minor

Tab Solos

CD #2
Track #2

Heavy Weight

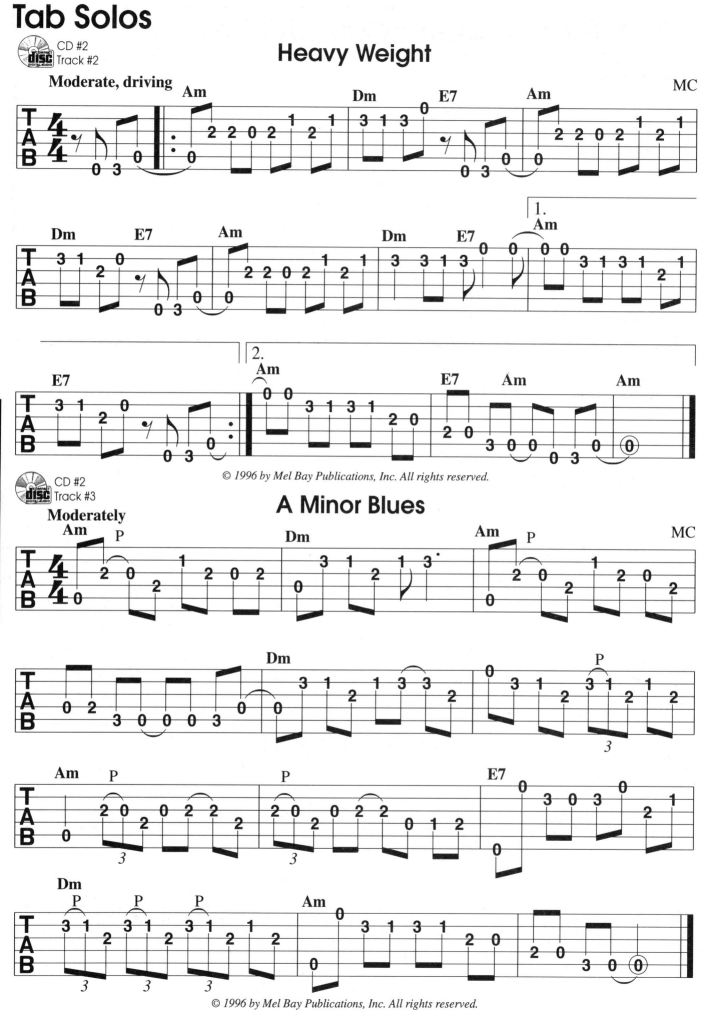

CD #2
Track #3

A Minor Blues

Key of A Minor

CD #2
Track #4

Interlude

WB

Slowly

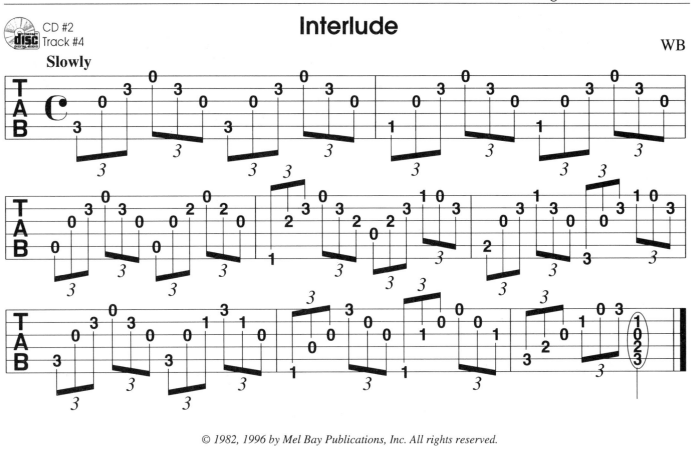

CD #2
Track #5

Cara's Farewell

WB

Driving Tempo, Rhythmically
Acc. Chords

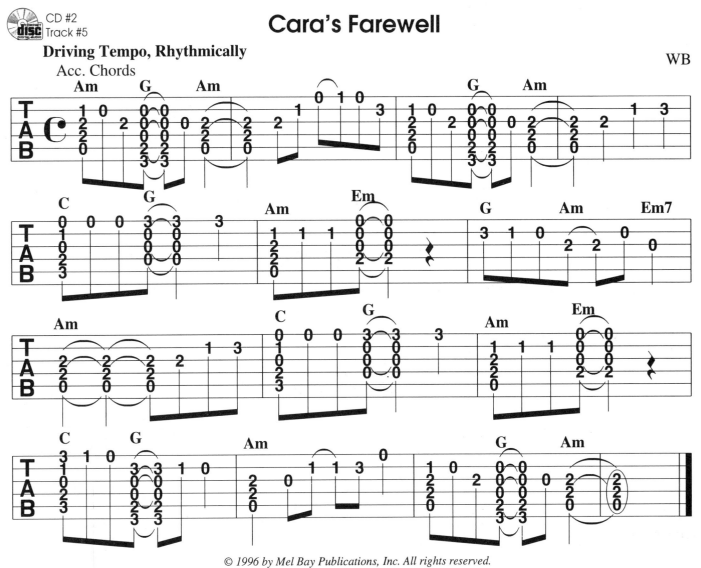

Tab Solos

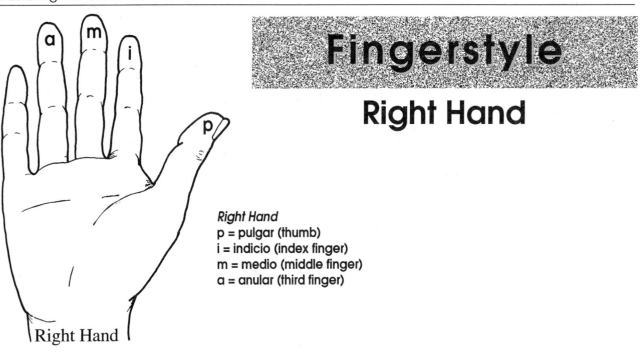

Fingerstyle

Right Hand

Right Hand
p = pulgar (thumb)
i = indicio (index finger)
m = medio (middle finger)
a = anular (third finger)

Right Hand

Fingerstyle

Playing Two or More Notes Together (Fingerstyle)

Before playing fingerstyle, an understanding of the right-hand position and type of strokes is necessary. Written below are the explanations of the *rest stroke* and *free stroke.*

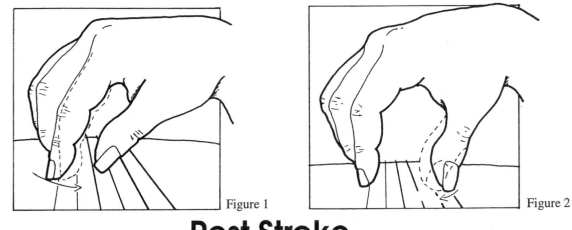

Figure 1

Figure 2

Rest Stroke

The rest stroke is commonly used to play melodies and is popular in solo guitar playing. To do the rest stroke, the flesh on the tip of the finger strokes the string is an upward (not outward) motion. The nail strokes the string as it passes by. *The finger then comes to rest on the next string (see figure 1).*

The thumb rest stroke is done by moving the thumb downward and playing the string with the tip of the thumb and the nail. The thumb then comes to rest on the next string down (see figure 2).

Spanish Dance

Use rest stroke on this study.

WB

Free Stroke

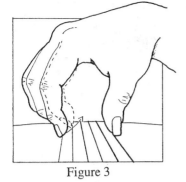

Figure 3

This is the stroke which is commonly used in accompaniment-style guitar playing. Because it allows the strings to ring, it is good for fingerpicking. It may also be used to play single note melodies. To do the free stroke, the finger picks the string and then is pulled out slightly *to avoid touching the next string.* Remember, it barely misses the next string. Do not pull away from the guitar too far or the string will slap (see figure 3).

The free stroke with the thumb is similar. After the thumb strokes the string, it is moved slightly outward to avoid hitting the next string (see figure 4).

Playing Two Notes Together

Figure 4

Generally, when music for the guitar is written in two parts, *the thumb plays the notes which have the stems going down and the fingers play the notes with the stems going up.* Each part (the fingers and the thumb) contains the correct number of beats to complete the measure. Therefore, the thumb part may have a rest while the fingers are playing and visa versa.

Play the following using a free stroke with the thumb and a rest stroke with the fingers (see rest and free stroke descriptions). The letters above or below the notes indicate which right-hand finger should be used to stroke the string.

Fingerstyle

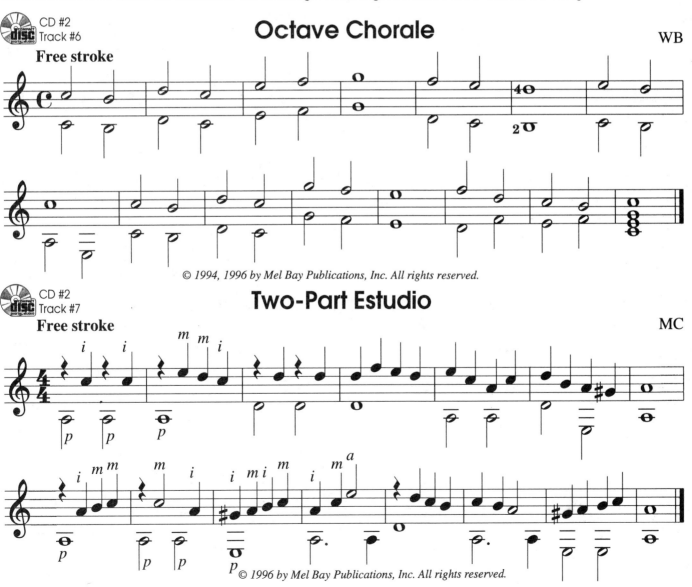

CD #2
Track #6

Octave Chorale

WB

Free stroke

CD #2
Track #7

Two-Part Estudio

MC

Free stroke

Practice the following solo with the thumb playing the lower notes and the finger playing the higher notes.

Trev and Tom

Fingerstyle Solo
Moderately fast

CD #2
Track #8

MC

Play the following arrangement of "Greensleeves." Be sure to hold the bass note (low note) for its total time value. A finger may have to be holding a bass note and allowing it to ring while the melody (upper notes) is moving.

Letters by the notes indicate which right-hand finger to use when picking the string. *Numbers indicate left-hand fingers and a circled number indicates the string on which that note is to be played.*

Greensleeves

Fingerstyle Solo
Moderately slow

CD #2
Track #9

MC

Fingerstyle

If the stems go down and up on a note, the note is played with the thumb, but is connected rhythmically to the other notes in the measure.

← Played with the thumb.

Practice the following solo in which some of the notes have double stems. Use free stroke.

Fingerstyle Solo

Estudio

CD #2
Track #10

D. Aguado

Play the following study with a pick and then with the right-hand fingers. Use free stroke.

Fingerstyle Solo

Allegro

CD #2
Track #11

M. Giuliani

Fingerstyle

Fingerstyle Solos

If more than two notes are played together fingerstyle, generally the thumb will play the lowest note and the fingers will play the upper notes. Be sure to have the notes sound at the same time.

Practice the following solo in which chords (more than two notes) are played fingerstyle. Use free stroke.

English Maiden

CD #2 Track #12

Fingerstyle Solo
Slowly

MC

allow this note to ring for 2 beats

Hold for 4 beats

Mexican Lament

CD #2 Track #13

Fingerstyle Solo
Slowly
Acc. Chords

WB

The Marsh of Rhuddlan

CD #2
Track #14

Fingerstyle Solo
Slowly
Acc. Chords

WB
Celtic Lament

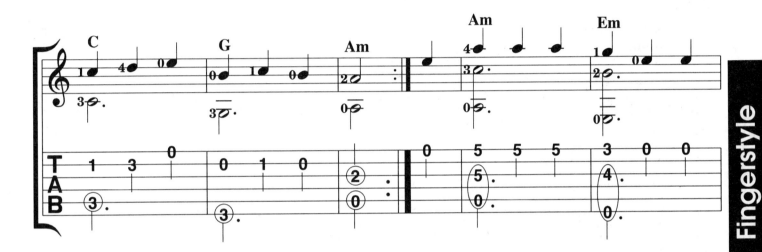

Fingerstyle

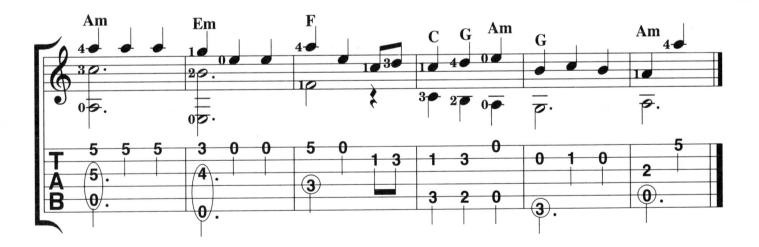

CD #2
Track #15

French Carol

WB

Fingerstyle Solo
Slowly

CD #2
Track #16

Picardy

WB
French Hymn

Fingerstyle Solo
Andante

CD #2
Track #17

St. James Infirmary

MC
Blues Solo

Fingerstyle Solo
Moderately

[Strum down
with Thumb]

Fingerstyle

CD #2
Track #18

Lonesome Blues

Fingerstyle Solo
Moderately

MC

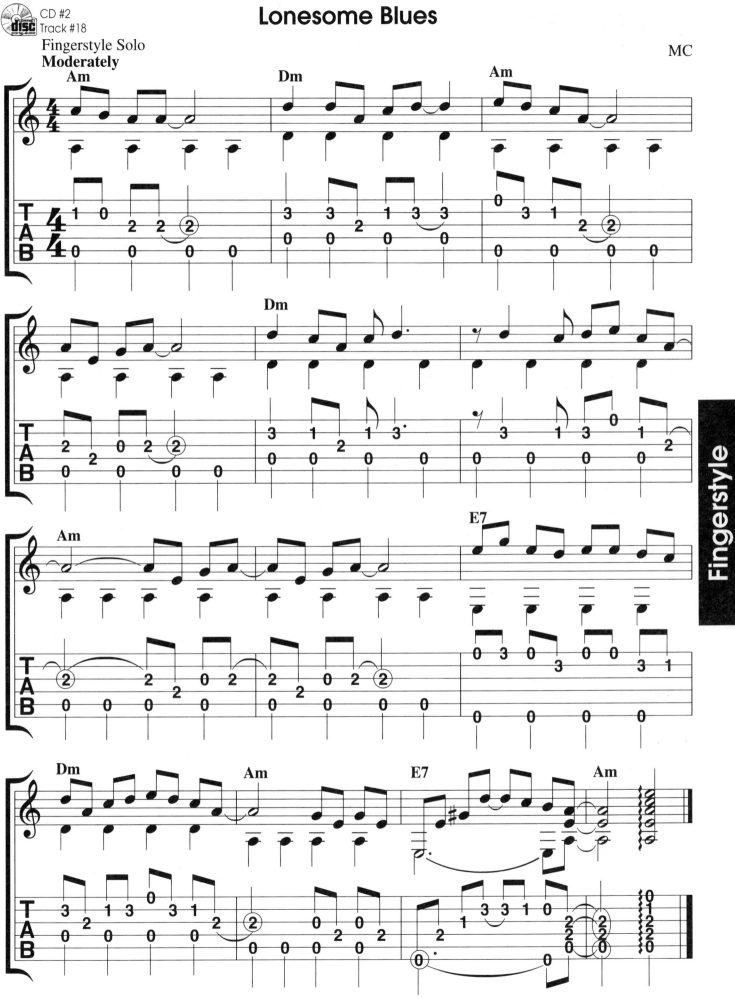

Fingerstyle

Chords in the Key of A minor

Written below are the primary chords in the key of A minor. The Roman numerals assigned to the chords are written below the chord names. The Roman numerals correspond to the steps of the A minor (the key) scale.

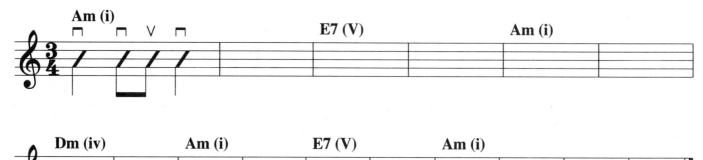

Am	Dm	E7
i	iv	V

Notice the i and iv chords are minor and the V chord is major (and usually a 7th chord) in a minor key.

Practice the following exercises and song which are in the key of A minor.

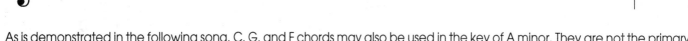

As is demonstrated in the following song, C, G, and F chords may also be used in the key of A minor. They are not the primary chords, but may be used.

Red Rocking Chair

Swing Rhythm

Normally when two eighth notes are connected together (♫) the beat is divided into two equal parts. When playing jazz and blues, it's more common to use **swing rhythm.** This means the first eighth note is longer than the second, so the beat is divided into a long–short pattern. With swing rhythm, two eighth notes are written the same but they are interpreted and played as a one-beat triplet with the middle note tied (♫ = 𝄽). Often, if the piece is to be played with swing rhythm this ♫ = 𝄽 will be written at the beginning of the music. Sometimes swing rhythm is also referred to as **shuffle rhythm.**

To get the swing feel, practice playing a single note over and over as in the example written below. First, play the eighth notes even and then swing them.

Next, practice playing the following scale and swing the eighth notes.

The rhythm will swing even more if you accent the off-beats. The example below shows where the accents would occur. Notice the accents come on the upstroke.

Another technique used to make the music swing and have a better jazz feel is to accent the notes which precede and follow rests. The example below shows where these accents would be placed.

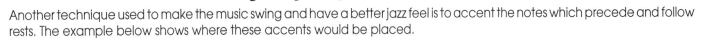

Practice playing the following blues solo and swing the eighth notes.

Flatpick Solo
Moderately (♫ = 𝄽)   **I Don't Know Why**   CD #2 Track #19   MC

Key of A Minor

Key Signatures

The *key signature* is the sharps or flats which are written at the beginning of the music and the beginning of each staff. The key signature indicates which notes (in every octave) should be sharp or flat throughout the entire piece. The letter names of the lines and spaces on which the sharps or flats are written in the key signature are the letter names of the notes to sharp or flat throughout the piece. For example, in the key signature shown at left, all of the F's and C's would be sharp. Not just the F's on the top line and the C's in the second space down...but all of the F's and C's. As with accidentals, a natural sign (♮) cancels a sharp or flat written in the key signature and is effective to the end of the measure.

Key of G

In the key of G we have one sharp – F♯. The key signature for G is:

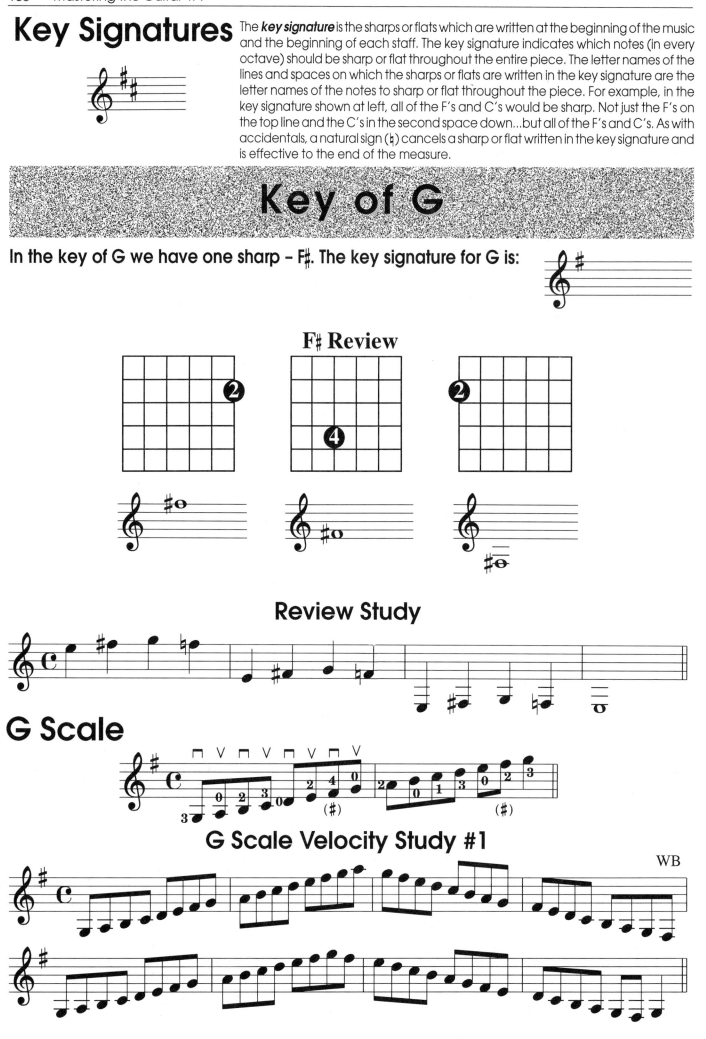

F♯ Review

Review Study

G Scale

G Scale Velocity Study #1

WB

G Scale Velocity Study #2

WB

G Scale Velocity Study #3

WB

G Scale Velocity Study #4

WB

Key of G

CD #2
Track #20

Same As You

Flatpick Solo
Slowly, let notes ring

MC

CD #2
Track #21

Flatt Shuffle

Flatpick Solo
Quickly

MC

* Remember A♯ is 1st Fret - 5th String

** Remember D♯ = 4th String
1st Fret

*** This A♯ is 3rd String
3rd Fret

Far From Home

CD #2
Track #22

WB
Shetland Island Reel

Flatpick Solo
Lively tempo
Acc. Chords **G**

CD #2
Track #23

On the Banks of that Lonely River

WB
Southern Mountain Ballad

Flatpick Solo
Slowly, with feeling
Acc. Chords **G**

Key of G

CD #2
Track #24

Slane

Flatpick Solo
Slowly
Acc. Chords

WB
Irish Hymn

CD #2
Track #25

Bransle Double

Flatpick Solo
Lively dance tempo
Acc. Chords

WB
Michael Praetorius

Key of G

CD #2
Track #26

Ballad

Flatpick Solo
Slowly

WB

CD #2
Track #27

Rondeau

Flatpick Solo
Moderately
Acc. Chords

WB
J. Mouret

CD #2
Track #28

Gavotte

Flatpick Solo
Rollicking, dance tempo

WB
M. Praetorius

D.S. 𝄋 al Fine

Key of G

Grace Notes

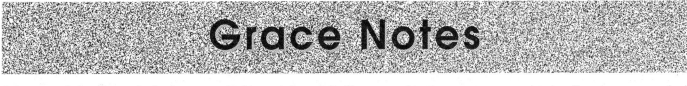

A **grace note** is a tiny note that appears before another note. There may be one or more grace notes. They are connected by a slur to the note they precede. Grace notes "borrow" their time value from the main note. Grace notes call for a quick hammer-on, pull-off, or combination of both. Grace notes are prevalent in Baroque music but also in Celtic, country, and bluegrass!

Grace Note Studies

The Flowers of Sweet Erin the Green

* Slide Review

The above solo used a slide. Remember, a slide is shown by a slanted line leading into a note. To play a slide, finger the note **two frets** below the desired note. Then, without lifting your finger, slide up to the correct pitch.

Key of G

The Teetotaller's Reel

Bury Me Beneath the Willow
Bluegrass TAB Solo

Key of G

Tab Solos

CD #2
Track #32

Salt Creek

Flatpick Solo

Lively

MC

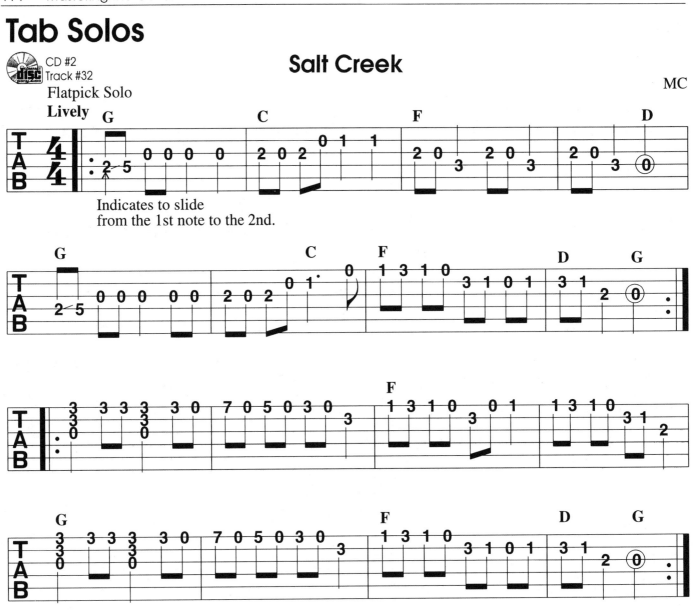

Indicates to slide
from the 1st note to the 2nd.

CD #2
Track #33

Memories Past

Flatpick Solo

Slowly, with feeling

Acc. Chords

WB

Key of G

Toll Free

Flatpick Solo
Moderately fast

Solos Using Syncopation

The following song, "Sugar in the Gourd," a fiddle tune, uses syncopation in the melody. Listen for the **accent** on the *up beat.*

Sugar in the Gourd

CD #2
Track #35   WB
Fiddle Tune

Flatpick Solo
Lively

Key of G

Washed in that Beautiful Pool

CD #2
Track #36

Flatpick Solo
Slow with a beat
Acc. Chords

WB
American Gospel Song

CD #2
Track #37

Gilotte

Flatpick Solo
Dance like
Acc. Chords

WB
Renaissance Dance

Key of G

Fingerpicking Solos

Fingerstyle Solo
Moderately slow

Silent Night

CD #2
Track #38

MC
Franz Gruber

Fingerstyle Solo
Acc. Chords

That Distant Shore

CD #2
Track #39

WB

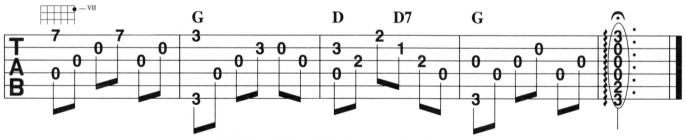

Key of G

CD #2
Track #40

The South Wind

Fingerstyle Solo

Slowly, Lyrically

Acc. Chords

WB
Irish

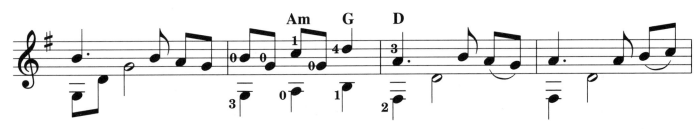

Key of G

Chords in the Key of G

Written below are the chords in the key of G. As with the key of C, notice the chord names go in scale order, and the I, IV, and V chords are major, while the ii, iii, and vi chords are minor.

G	Am	Bm	C	D(7)	Em
I	ii	iii	IV	V	vi

Practice the following exercises which use chords from the key of G. In each exercise, continue playing the strum pattern which is written in the first measure.

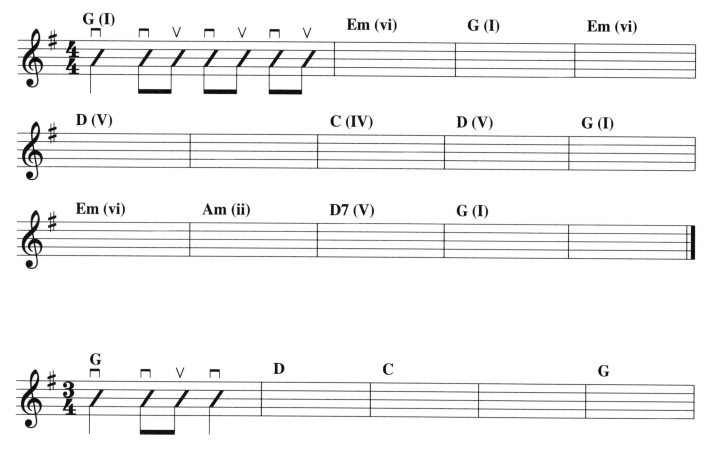

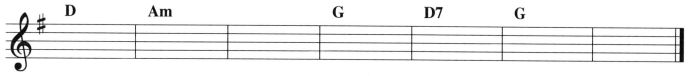

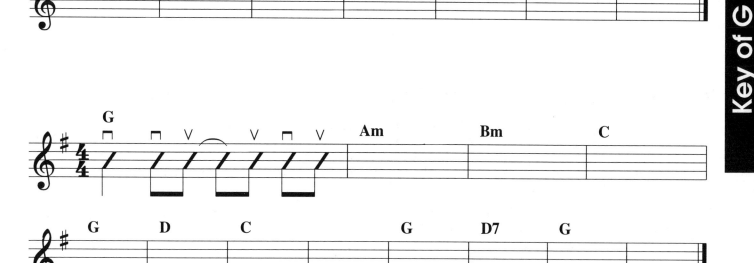

Key of G

Practice playing the chords to the following song which uses chords in the key of G. Use the strum pattern written above the first measure to play each measure of the song.

Silent Night

Franz Grüber

Gently

Si - lent night, ho - ly night,

All is calm, all is bright,

Round yon vir - gin moth - er and child.

Ho - ly in - fant so ten - der and mild,

Sleep in heav - en - ly peace, _____

Sleep _____ in heav - en - ly peace. _____

Fingerpicking Patterns

A popular type of accompaniment is called **pattern picking.** Pattern picking refers to holding a chord and fingerpicking the strings in an order which is then repeated in each measure. To learn these fingerpicking patterns, divide the chords into three categories; 6-string, 5-string, and 4-string chords. The category for a particular chord is determined by how many strings are played when the chord is strummed. For example, G would be a 6-string chord because all six strings are played when a G chord is strummed.

The chart at right shows a fingerpicking pattern which can be used to accompany songs in 4/4 time. Each pattern takes one measure to complete. The patterns are shown using tablature. As in standard tablature, the six lines represent the guitar strings. Rather than placing numbers on the lines, letters are used. These letters represent the traditional Spanish naming of the right-hand fingers:

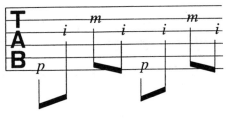

p = pulgar (thumb)
i = indicio (index finger)
m = medio (middle finger)
a = anular (third finger)

When a letter is placed on a line, play that string with the finger indicated by the letter. The stems on the letters indicate the rhythm. For example, hold a G chord and play the following patterns:

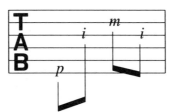

In the pattern above, a G chord is held and the sixth string is picked with the right-hand thumb, the third string is picked with the index finger, the second string is picked with the middle finger, and the third string is picked with the index finger. This pattern could be used to play any six-string chord (i.e., G, G7, Em, E7, etc.). So, for example, the same pattern could be used for Em that is used for G because both chords are 6-string chords.

Generally, when doing fingerpick patterns, the right-hand thumb will play strings 6, 5, and 4. The right-hand fingers (i, m, and a) will play strings 1, 2, and 3. Written below is a fingerpicking pattern which can be used to accompany songs in 4/4. Each pattern takes one measure to complete. The pattern for the 6-string chords is written on the left. The pattern for 5-string chords is shown in the middle, and the 4-string pattern is on the right. Notice the right-hand finger order stays the same for each pattern.

6 - string chords (i.e. G, Em)   5 - string chords (i.e. C, Am)   4 - string chords (i.e. D, F)

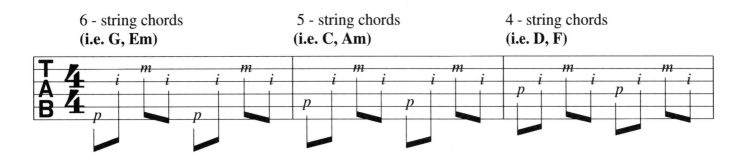

Practice the following exercises using this fingerpicking pattern. The patterns are written in the first of each chord. Normally, the fingerpick patterns are not written in the music. These patterns should be memorized and then, depending on whether the chord written is a 6-, 5-, or 4-string, the correct pattern should be used. After playing this exercise, go back to earlier songs and exercises in this book and apply this fingerpicking pattern.

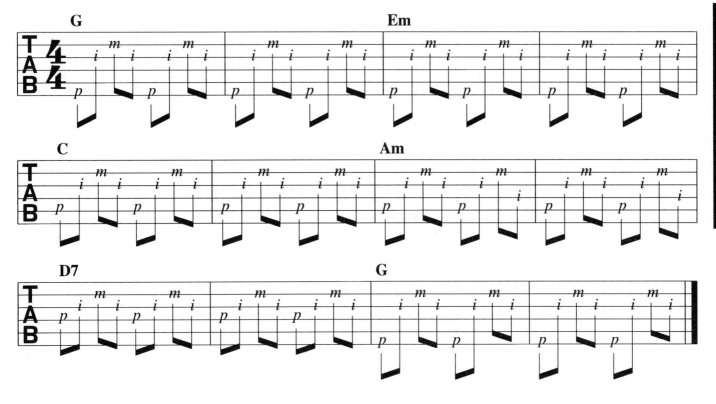

Play the following song using the previously shown fingerpick pattern. Remember, many other songs may be played using this fingerpicking pattern. To help get started, the fingerpick pattern has been written on the tablature, under the melody. To play the correct pattern for each chord, see if the chord is a 6-, 5-, or 4-string chord and then play the pattern which applies to that particular chord.

The Water Is Wide

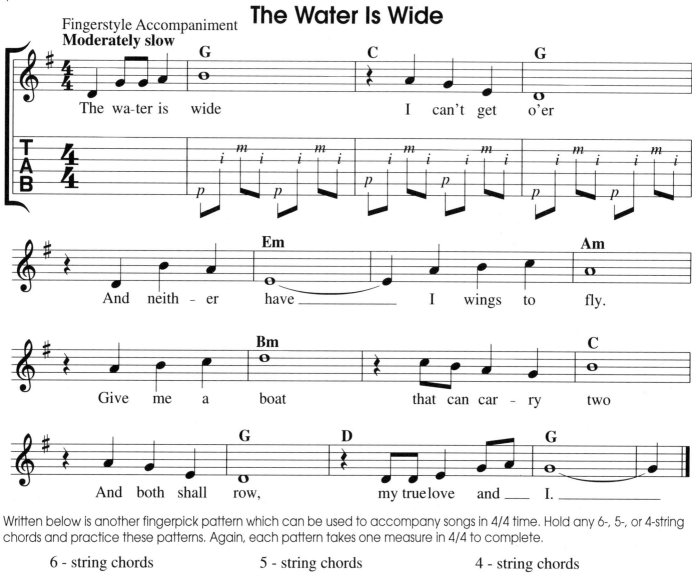

Written below is another fingerpick pattern which can be used to accompany songs in 4/4 time. Hold any 6-, 5-, or 4-string chords and practice these patterns. Again, each pattern takes one measure in 4/4 to complete.

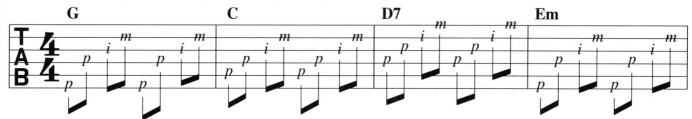

Practice the following exercise using this new fingerpick pattern for 4/4.

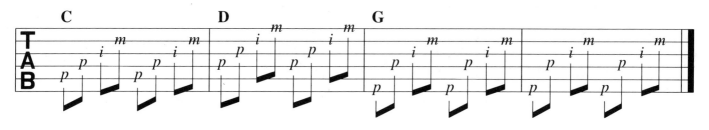

Practice the following song using the new pattern for 4/4. As a rule, if two chords appear in a measure (each chord getting two beats), divide the fingerpick pattern in half. Again, to get started the fingerpick pattern has been written for the first line under the melody. Depending on whether the chord for the measure is a 6-, 5-, or 4-string chord, play the correct pattern.

Three Ravens

E Minor

In the key of E minor we have one sharp – F#. Thus, the key of E minor is "relative" to the key of G major.

E Natural Minor Scale

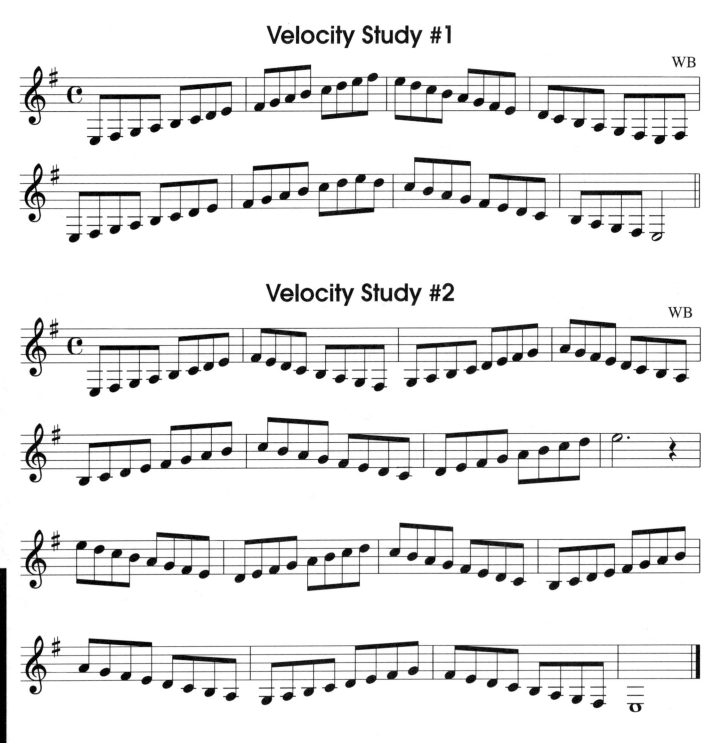

E Harmonic Minor

In the E Harmonic Minor Scale, the 7th scale tone – D – is sharped. D♯ is a common note when playing in the key of E minor.

D♯ Note Review

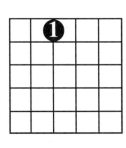

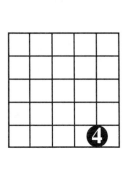

E Harmonic Minor Scale

Velocity Study #1

WB

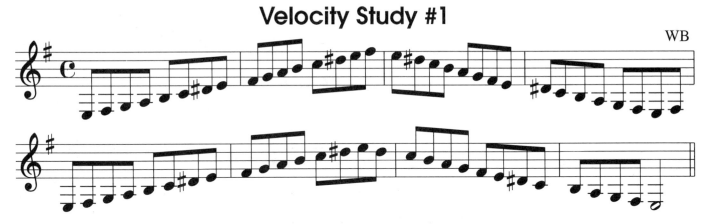

Velocity Study #2

WB

Key of E minor

Jamaican Shoreline

Flatpick Solo
Moderately fast

CD #2
Track #41

MC

Buena Vista

Flatpick Solo
Slow, flowing

CD #2
Track #42

WB

Fine

D.S. % al Fine

Shabat Shalom
(Song for the Sabbath)

Flatpick Solo
Gently

CD #2
Track #43

WB
Hebrew

Fine

D.S. % al Fine

Key of E minor

Room 124

CD #2
Track #44

Flatpick Solo
Moderate, driving

MC

Last time, go from here
to the coda ($\oplus$) – in this
piece, the last measure.

To Coda $\oplus$

rit.

Go to the D.S. sign ($\%$) and play to
the "to coda" (to ending) sign ($\oplus$).

D.S. $\%$ *al Coda* $\oplus$

$\oplus$ *Coda*

1/2

Key of E minor

Shaker Dance

CD #2
Track #45

WB

Flatpick Solo
Moderately, with rhythmic feeling

Johnny Has Gone For A Soldier

In this beautiful ballad we have a fermata (𝄐). When this sign occurs hold the note or notes under the sign for an extended period of time.

WB
Civil War Ballad

CD #2
Track #46

Flatpick Solo
Slowly, with free expression

fade volume

pp

XX O

* Bm

Key of E minor

House of the Rising Sun

Use pick or fingers.

Key of E minor

Six-Eight Time

This sign  indicates six-eight time.

6 – beats per measure
8 – type of note receiving one beat

An eighth note ♪ = one beat, a quarter note ♩ = two beats, a dotted quarter note ♩. = three beats, and a sixteenth note ♬ = 1/2 beat.

Six-eight time consists of two units containing three beats each.

It will be counted: with the accents on beats one and four.
1- 2- 3- 4- 5- 6

Here are two Irish jigs. Watch for the C♯ notes. They are fun to play as duets. Have your teacher or another guitarist play the chords and rhythm while you play the melody.

Swallowtail Jig

Flatpick Solo
Moderately
Acc. Chords

CD #2
Track #49

WB
Irish Jig

Morrison's Jig

Flatpick Solo
Moderately
Acc. Chords

CD #2
Track #50

WB
Irish Jig

Key of E minor

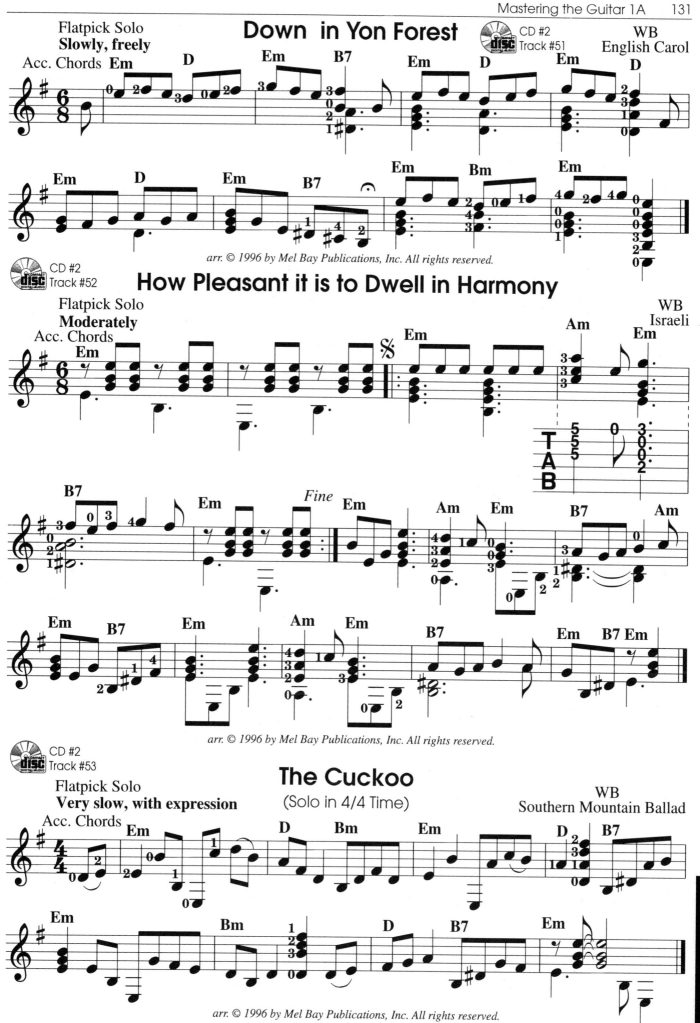

Down in Yon Forest

Flatpick Solo
Slowly, freely
Acc. Chords

CD #2 Track #51

WB
English Carol

CD #2 Track #52

How Pleasant it is to Dwell in Harmony

Flatpick Solo
Moderately
Acc. Chords

WB
Israeli

CD #2 Track #53

The Cuckoo

(Solo in 4/4 Time)

Flatpick Solo
Very slow, with expression
Acc. Chords

WB
Southern Mountain Ballad

Key of E minor

The Clergy's Lamentation

Flatpick Solo
Moderately

CD #2
Track #54

WB
Turlough O'Carolan

Tambourin

Flatpick Solo
Allegro

CD #2
Track #55

WB
Rameau

Two New Notes

The following solos use High B and High C.

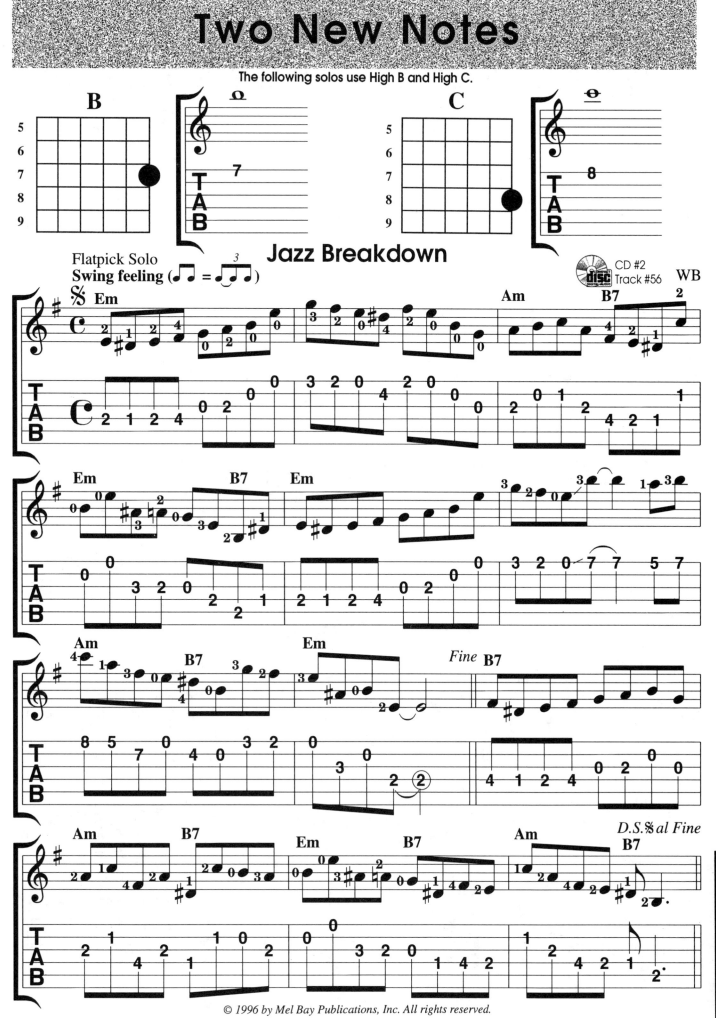

Jazz Breakdown

Flatpick Solo
Swing feeling

CD #2
Track #56   WB

Key of E minor

Tango Guitarra

CD #2
Track #57

WB

Flatpick Solo
Tango rhythm

Alternate B7

CD #2
Track #58

Three Past Midnight

WB

Flatpick Solo
Steady, Rock beat

Key of E minor

Fingerpicking Solos
O Come, O Come Emmanuel

CD #2
Track #59

MC

Fingerstyle Solo

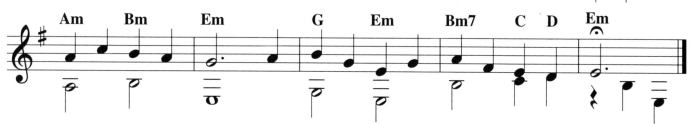

Ashley's Song

CD #2
Track #60

Fingerstyle Solo
Moderately slow

MC

Key of E minor

CD #2
Track #61

Casa de Grout

Habanera
MC

Fingerstyle Solo
Moderately, habanera rhythm

CD #2
Track #62

In the Pines

Fingerstyle Solo
Slow blues
Acc. Chords

WB

Lord Randal

CD #2 Track #63

WB Appalachian Ballad

Fingerstyle Solo
Slowly

CD #2 Track #64

Half Past Midnight

Fingerstyle Solo
Moderate blues feeling

MC

Key of E minor

CD #2
Track #65

Andante

Flatpick or Fingerstyle   Play with fingers and also with a flatpick.

Moderately, flowing

Carcassi

Minuet
(Duet)

WB
J. S. Bach

Key of E minor

CD #2
Track #67

Bahía Tranquilo

(Solo Or Duet)

WB

Key of E minor

Chords in the Key of E Minor

The primary chords for the key of E minor are written below. The Roman numeral assignments for the chords are written below the chord names.

Em	Am	B7
i	iv	V

Practice the following exercises using the chords in the key of E minor.

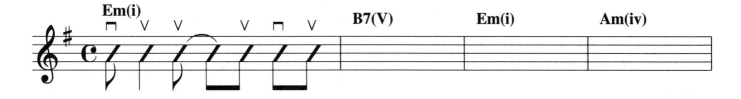

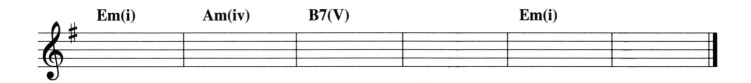

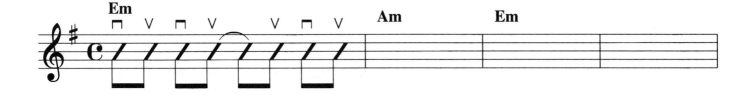

Practice the following songs which are in E minor. In "House of the Rising Sun," other chords in E minor in addition to the primary chords have been used.

A Poor Wayfaring Stranger

Anon

I'm   just   a   poor _____ way - far - ing

stran - ger. __ A trav-lin' through __ this world of woe _____ But there's no

sick   -   ness, toil or dan - ger __ In that bright world _____ to which I

go. _____ I'm go - ing there _____ to meet my Fa - ther __ I'm go - ing

there _____ no more to roam _____ I'm just a go - ing __ o - ver __

Jor - dan _____ I'm just a go   -   ing o - ver home.

In the following song, the chords may be strummed or the tablature may be played with a pick or fingerpicked.

House of the Rising Sun

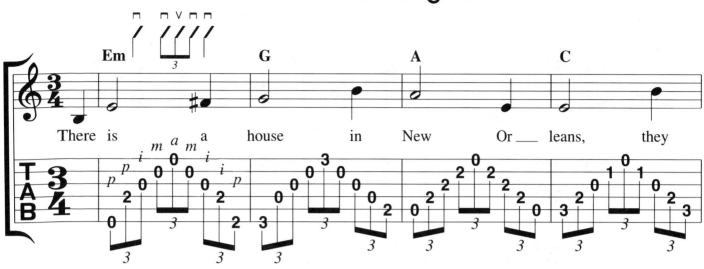

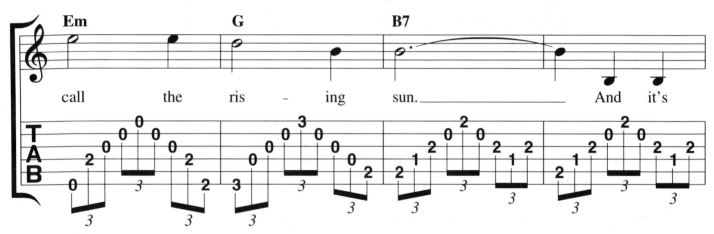

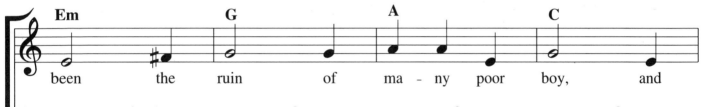

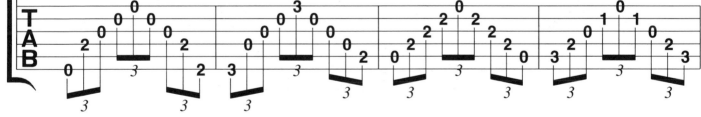

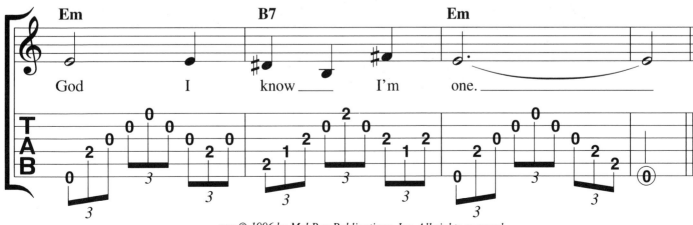

Key of E minor

Congratulations for finishing Book 1A!!!

*Don't stop now.
You've only just begun.*

*You are now ready
to proceed to
Mastering the Guitar
Book 1B.*